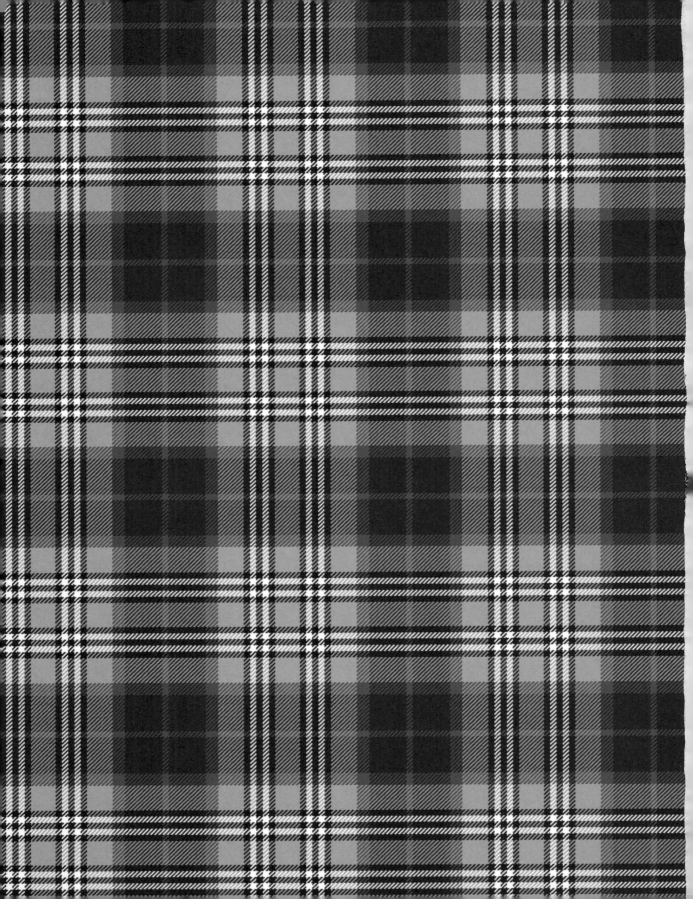

Tailored
for
Scotland

Deirdre Kinloch Anderson

DEDICATIONS

This book is dedicated to all of my eight grandchildren. They are, in order of date of birth: Douglas, Catriona, Lachie, Ameline, Annie, Harris, Isobel and Ruth – and each one of them has Kinloch as a middle name. They are growing into fine people and I am so proud of them all.

It is far too soon to know which of them, if any, might find fulfilment in their life by using their qualifications and their talents in order to develop the company and move Kinloch Anderson into the seventh generation.

In April 2020, at the time when this book was in its last stages of completion, my brother-in-law, Sir Eric Kinloch Anderson, sadly passed away. He was renowned as an English scholar, headmaster and educationalist, and I also wish to dedicate this book to his memory. Some of the outstanding contributions to our country that Eric made in his remarkable life are featured later in this book. However, for me, one of his greatest legacies will always be the positive influence that he had on the lives of so many young people, not only those who were to become great and famous but those many others whose daily deeds remain unsung.

First published 2020 by Waverley Books, an imprint of The Gresham Publishing Company Ltd, 31, Six Harmony Row, Glasgow, G51 3BA, Scotland, UK.

www.waverley-books.co.uk
info@waverley-books.co.uk
facebook/pages/waverleybooks

ISBN 978-1-84934-531-6

Printed and bound in China.

CONTENTS

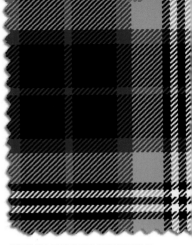

CITY OF EDINBURGH TARTAN

Book cover, endpapers and swatch above:
The City of Edinburgh tartan was designed by Kinloch Anderson to mark the Commonwealth Heads of Government Meeting, hosted by the City of Edinburgh in October 1997.

The sett for the tartan is based on the Stewart Old Clan Tartan because of the City's kinship with the Stewarts over many centuries.

The colours of the design are based on the Arms of the City of Edinburgh Council.

Front endpaper: North Bridge Street, by Swarbreck, Samuel Dunkinfield, 1837.

ABOUT THE AUTHOR

DEIRDRE Anne Kinloch Anderson (née Loryman) came to Scotland in order to study French and Spanish at St Andrews University. There she met Douglas, whom she married just one year after her graduation. Looking back over her early married years, this was the time when Douglas was running the company together with his father whilst Deirdre was running the family and the household. Their roles were complementary but very different. Deirdre is known to have reasoned that motherhood is good training for business. "You learn to make quick decisions in times of crisis, to do several things at once, to cope with constant interruptions, to put others' interests first, to use the art of persuasion, to be tolerant and, not least, to listen as well as to talk," she says.

For her, motherhood gave an opportunity to understand and to guide the development of her children and to instil a love of learning through reading books.

Douglas Kinloch Anderson was a frequent traveller to the USA, Europe and the Far East whilst Deirdre chose to be at home for her children when they came back from school. Except in the teaching profession, the employment market was not really structured to accommodate the requirements and demands of motherhood at that time. Mobile phones and computers were yet to be become available to assist this process.

In 1990, when the children had left school, Deirdre joined Kinloch Anderson as "leaflet delivery girl". She was to take her time to embrace the complexities and the challenges of the company's ever-widening activities. Never taking her position for granted, she once said, "When entering a family business, one of the greatest challenges is to establish yourself and your ability in your own right and not just as a privileged family member."

She has worked and taken responsibility in all the divisions of the company,

Page 5 and swatch above: The Kinloch Anderson tartan was the first of the specially designed Kinloch Anderson Tartan Collection. The Scottish surname of Anderson means "son of Andrew", and Kinloch was the middle name of two sons of the company's founder and is still included in the family name of all generations to the present day.

Every Kinloch Anderson tartan has been based on the clan Anderson tartan sett (pattern), and each one tells its own story. The Kinloch Anderson tartan colours of navy, muted green and burgundy reflect the classic, timeless nature of the company, whilst black and gold identify with the Kinloch Anderson brand logo.

Above left: Deirdre Kinloch Anderson, OBE.

given hands-on demonstrations of kiltmaking and writes and interviews for magazines, press and TV. Her contribution to society and the workplace has extended well beyond the confines of the company. A businesswoman at heart, she lost no time in widening her interests.

She was President of the Leith Chamber of Commerce, Member of the Governing Body of Queen Margaret University College, Fellow of the Royal Society of Arts, Companion of the Institute of Membership and Member of the Master's Court of the Merchant Company. In 1998 she was the first lady to be asked to join the Society of High Constables of the City of Edinburgh. This society was founded in 1611 and she remained a member for twenty years.

No introduction to Deirdre Kinloch Anderson would be complete without mention of the word tartan, that great Scottish symbol of identity that has always been at the very heart of the Kinloch Anderson profile, its past heritage and its future potential.

Below: Three generations of Kinloch Andersons wearing their Anderson tartan kilts at the "Gathering of the Clans" event, in Holyrood Park, Edinburgh, 2009.

Life & times

Tartan tigress Deirdre gets OBE for services to textiles

Deirdre's passionate interest in tartan is holistic. She appreciates how the influence of tartan – which she insists belongs to culture and not to science – has endured to the present day. It has real significance in anchoring the identity of individuals, families, districts, companies, organisations, societies and for commemorating special events. Tartan belongs to the people of Scotland and as they have migrated overseas they have taken their tartans with them. "Tartan is a gift that Scotland has given to the world," she says.

Deirdre has strong views about the pride with which it should be worn. She has even been nicknamed the "Tartan Tigress" which maybe tells you something about her character!

With persistence and commitment over seven years, she was instrumental in the establishment of the Scottish Register of Tartans in 2009. Tartan registration is now in the public domain within the National Archives of Scotland and the individual identity and integrity of each tartan is safeguarded in perpetuity. In recognition of her efforts, she was awarded an OBE in 2010 for her contribution to the textile industry.

Foreword
DAVID KINLOCH ANDERSON
LORD ANDERSON OF IPSWICH KBE QC

T HE Kinloch Anderson company was a strong presence during my Edinburgh childhood. Though my parents were at one remove from the business, which was run at the time by my grandfather and my uncle, Douglas, the family (as befits its trade) is a close-knit one.

So it was that I learned the tartans from a gigantic book of cloth samples, had kilts fitted in the George Street sanctum, marvelled at computerised machines in the Restalrig factory, and – a less happy memory – assisted my grandfather by demonstrating to an amused Women's Rural in the Highlands, aged thirteen and in my underwear, the art of rolling into a plaid.

Life took me on a different journey: but it seemed natural, when making my maiden speech in the House of Lords, to express my pride in a company then celebrating its 150th year in the sixth generation of family management.

The secret of that rare longevity is told in this book. Royal patronage, military heritage and a tradition of service are fine assets: but a small business must also anticipate the future. The survival and growth of Kinloch Anderson have been the result of a series of prescient decisions, from embracing ready-to-wear in the 1920s to building brands and markets in the twenty-first century Far East.

This beautifully-researched and illustrated book is the story not just of a unique Scottish company but of the family that gave it life and the times in which it has lived. I wish it every success.

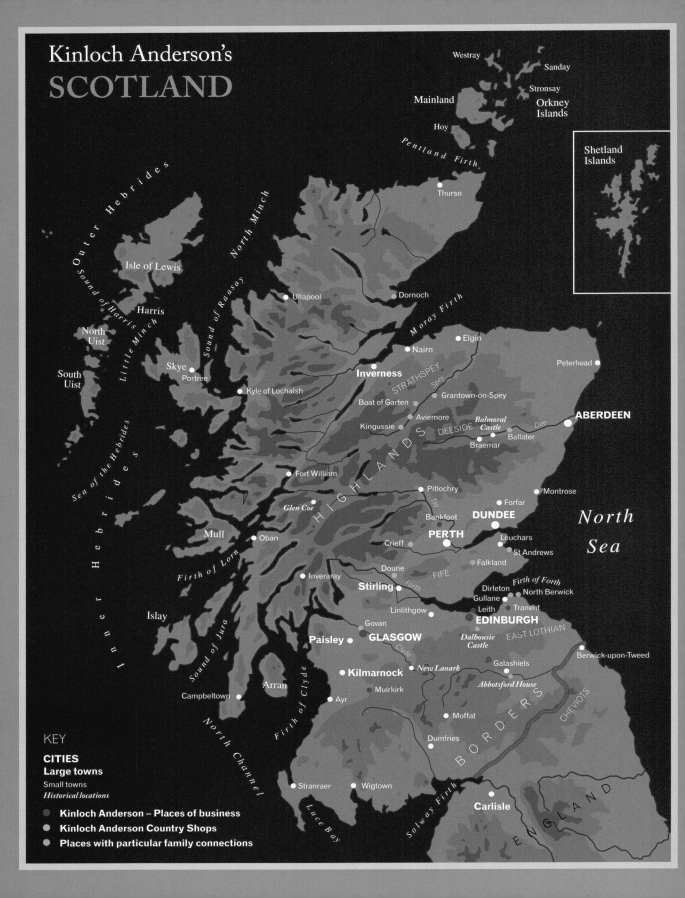

Kinloch Anderson's
SCOTLAND

Westray

Sanday

Mainland

Stronsay

Orkney
Islands

Hoy

Pentland Firth

Shetland
Islands

Thurso

Outer Hebrides

North Minch

Ullapool

Dornoch

Moray Firth

Elgin

Peterhead

Isle of Lewis

Sound of Raasay

Nairn

North Uist

Harris

Little Minch

Skye

Inverness

STRATHSPEY

Spey

Grantown-on-Spey

Dee

ABERDEEN

South
Uist

Portree

Kyle of Lochalsh

Boat of Garten

Aviemore

HIGHLANDS

DEESIDE

Balmoral Castle

Sea of the Hebrides

Kingussie

Braemar

Ballater

Inner Hebrides

Fort William

Pitlochry

Montrose

Glen Coe

Forfar

Mull

Oban

Bankfoot

Tay

DUNDEE

*North
Sea*

Firth of Lorn

Crieff

PERTH

Leuchars

St Andrews

Doune

Falkland

FIFE

Inveraray

Forth

Stirling

Firth of Forth

Dirleton

Islay

Linlithgow

Gullane

North Berwick

Govan

Leith

Tranent

GLASGOW

EDINBURGH

Arran

Paisley

Clyde

*Dalhousie
Castle*

EAST LOTHIAN

Kilmarnock

New Lanark

Galashiels

Berwick-upon-Tweed

Campbeltown

Muirkirk

Abbotsford House

CHEVIOTS

Ayr

BORDERS

Moffat

Sound of Jura

Firth of Clyde

North Channel

Dumfries

Stranraer

Wigtown

ENGLAND

Luce Bay

Solway Firth

Carlisle

KEY

CITIES
Large towns
Small towns
Historical locations

- Kinloch Anderson – Places of business
- Kinloch Anderson Country Shops
- Places with particular family connections

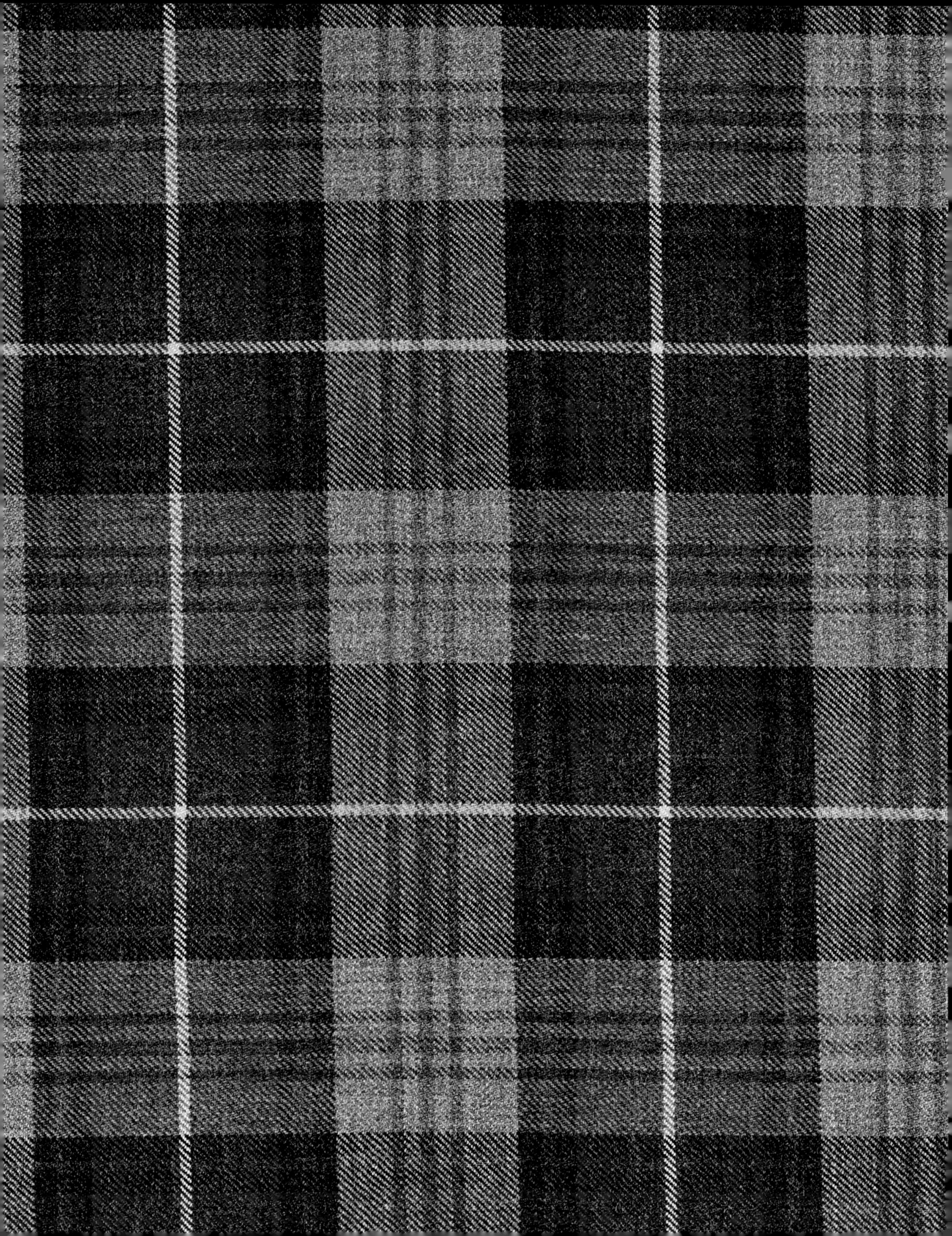

Above: Edinburgh from Calton Hill
Painted by Birket Foster

HISTORICAL BACKGROUND

KINLOCH ANDERSON
CASTLE GREY TARTAN

I T SEEMS a remarkable coincidence that the 150th anniversary of the Kinloch Anderson Company in 2018 was exactly 200 years from 1818, the date of the birth of William Anderson, founder of William Anderson & Sons Limited in 1868, in Edinburgh.

The City of Edinburgh – the home of the old Scottish kings and nobility, the capital of Scotland, with its castle and palace and the Royal Mile between, and where every stone has a legend attached to it – has seen enormous change in the past 200 years.

This volume, *Tailored for Scotland*, tells the story of the Kinloch Anderson Company. It draws on Edinburgh's history, beginning in the century that gave us William Anderson and bringing with it many outstanding achievements and events to which the citizens of the time were hugely indebted – and indeed to which Edinburgh and Scotland remain indebted today. Writers, artists, craftsmen, pioneer town planners, town council representatives and other business professionals, have been recognised for some of the greatest innovations and developments that took place all these years ago.

The nineteenth century was a hugely progressive period that affected all aspects of life in Edinburgh. The first half of the century, called "the Awakening of Edinburgh"*, followed the period of the Scottish Enlightenment and the city did indeed awake and set out on a path of progress in trade and commerce, much of which formed the basis for continued development in present times.

When James VI rode south in 1603 to be King of England as well as of Scotland, Edinburgh suffered greatly on account of the absence of the Court. It was even harder hit when its ancient Parliament was abolished in 1707, followed by an exodus of the Scottish nobility from the capital and the country itself. For the first half of the eighteenth century, the city made little or no progress. A deep sleep had fallen upon it, from which it was only

Page 11 and swatch above: Kinloch Anderson has been based in Edinburgh, the capital of Scotland, since 1868, and Edinburgh Castle is the city's most famous historic monument. The Kinloch Anderson Castle Grey tartan has three shades of grey which represent the castle rocks, and the red overcheck relates to the City of Edinburgh's Coat of Arms.

Edinburgh in the Nineteenth Century, Ed. WM Gilbert.

fitfully disturbed by the events of the Rebellion of 1715, the Porteous mob riots twenty-one years later, and the few days of celebration when the "Old Pretender" James Edward Stuart (1688–1766) was proclaimed King at the Mercat Cross, Edinburgh on September 16, 1745.

In 1800, the whole of Europe was up in arms against Napoleon. By sea and land, Britain was fighting France in her struggle for supremacy, which was not to end until fifteen years later on the field of Waterloo. Describing the New Town of Edinburgh in 1800, a contemporary writer, declared:

> It has three streets almost a mile in length, running from east to west, intersected with cross-streets at proper distances. The most northerly, called Queen Street, is 100 feet broad and commands an extensive prospect of the Forth, the county of Fife and the shipping on the river. That called George Street, which is in the middle, is no less than 115 feet wide. It is terminated at each end by two very elegant and extensive squares; that on the east end is called St Andrew Square, the other, Charlotte Square. Princes Street is the most southerly and extends from the northern extremity of the bridge to the west end of the town; Nicolson's Street, itself making now one street with the South and North Bridges and having the front of the Register Office in full view at the northern end of the last of these Bridges, forms a part of perhaps the most interesting street in the whole town or in almost any part of Britain.

The coronation of George IV, took place in July 1821. As monarch of Great Britain and Ireland, he was able to give full reign to his flamboyant and romantic tendencies. He always took great interest in the garments that he wore and cultivated the popular idea that His Majesty was the "last word" in the realm of fashion. His coronation in July 1821 was itself an occasion of extreme pomp and magnificence. He led an extravagant lifestyle that contributed to the fashions of the Regency era and was a patron of new forms of style and taste.

In August 1822, George IV made a state visit to Scotland, this being the first occasion that Scotland had been so honoured since the days of the Stuarts.

Walter Scott was the mastermind of King George's Scottish visit. After George's accession to the throne, the City Council had invited Scott, at the King's behest, to manage the visit. Scott is one of Scotland's most highly esteemed Scottish writers. He was awarded the freedom of the city for his literary talents in 1818. Scott's explorations and interpretations of Scottish history and society captured popular imagination. In March 1820 he became Sir Walter Scott – a hugely popular accolade.

> The citizens read with great satisfaction the announcement in the Gazette of April 1st that the King had made Mr Walter Scott of Abbotsford a baronet. Sir Walter was the first baronet created after the King's accession.

Scott's influential Scottish romantic novels travelled far and wide, and his writings not only transformed literary culture but changed how the world viewed Scotland.

In 1822, Scott created a spectacular and comprehensive pageant, designed not only to impress the King, but which healed the rifts that had destabilised society in Scotland. The King's journey began when he embarked for the north at Greenwich. The nation learned of his departure and, of course, what he was wearing. "He wore a blue coat and foraging cap, his trousers were white and his boots were 'a la Wellington'."

The King's ship, the *Royal George*, arrived in the Firth of Forth around noon on Wednesday August 14, but his landing was postponed for two days due to torrential rain. Despite the rain, Sir Walter Scott went out to the Royal Yacht. When it was announced to the King that Scott was alongside, he exclaimed, "Sir Walter Scott! The man in Scotland I most wished to see. Let him come up." After a toast with Glenlivet whisky in the name of the ladies of Scotland, Scott presented the King with a handsome badge in the form of a St Andrew's cross, embroidered with pearls on blue velvet with a belt of gold, a diamond buckle and magnificent Scottish pearl surmounted by the imperial crown, picked out in brilliants, rubies, emeralds and topaz. Inscribed on the cross was: "*Righ Albainn gu brath*" translated as "Long life for the King".

The King landed at Leith on August 16, when all the authorities, officers of the Crown and many noblemen met him and joined in a grand procession to Dalhousie Castle. Contrary to what you may have seen in some pictures, he did not wear Highland costume until the next day. "When His Majesty

Left: Detail from a painting by Alexander Carse showing King George IV landing on the Shore at Leith in 1822. The main building is the Custom House on the opposite bank of the Water of Leith.

came ashore he wore the full dress uniform of an admiral, with St Andrew's cross and a large thistle in his gold-laced hat." The King mounted his carriage, saluted by cavalry and Highland Infantry and the Gentlemen Archers of the Royal Guard, and so he entered Edinburgh. Sir Walter Scott had grasped the opportunity to create a pageant in which ancient Scotland could be reborn.

A levee was held the following day at Holyrood Palace which the Scottish nobility attended in full force. As a graceful compliment to the national feeling, "The King wore the Highland costume, selecting the tartan of the Stuarts as the colour of his dress." He wanted to win the loyalty of the Scottish people and Walter Scott persuaded His Majesty not only that he was as much a Stuart as Bonnie Prince Charlie, but also that he was a Jacobite Highlander and so could properly wear "the Garb of Old Gaul" which he did, in a Highland outfit complete with "gold chains, dirk, swords and pistols." A local contemporary newspaper *The Edinburgh Star* gave details of the costume worn at that function:

> On this occasion, no gentleman can appear otherwise than in full dress suit, with sword and bag; but hair powder is not now held to be indispensable. Gentlemen may appear in any uniform to which they have a right and, for those who present themselves as Highlanders, the ancient costume of their country is always sufficient dress. Those who wear the Highland Dress must, however, be careful to be armed in the proper Highland fashion – steel-wrought pistols, broadsword and dirk. It is understood that Glengarry, Breadalbane, Huntly and several other chieftains mean to attend the levee, "with their tail on", i.e. with a considerable attendance of their gentlemen followers.

The Edinburgh Star also relates:

> *Since the period when James VI left Scotland to assume the sceptre of the United Kingdom, Edinburgh has not been visited by any Sovereign in the full and undisturbed enjoyment of regal splendour and power. Charles II is the only king who has ever seen it.*
>
> *The King attended splendid banquets, the High Church, the Caledonian Hunt Ball, the Theatre and he visited Melville Castle, Newbattle Abbey and finally Hopetoun House. The visit has been called "One and Twenty Daft Days".*

There was widespread concern about procedure and etiquette for these banquets, levees and public appearances, not least amongst the Highland Chiefs and their followers. Scott addressed this by producing a shilling booklet "Hints addressed to the inhabitants of Edinburgh and others in prospect of His Majesty's Visit. By an old citizen". This booklet gave an outline of planned events with detailed advice on behaviour and clothing.

All gentlemen of the city were expected to attend public appearances in a uniform blue coat, white waistcoat and white or nankeen (cream) cotton trousers and a low-crowned dark hat decorated with a cockade in the form of a white St Andrew's saltire on a blue background. Similarly, detailed guidance was given for those fortunate enough to attend functions or levees, with gentlemen to wear a full dress suit. Indeed, everyone was expected to "add greatly to the variety, gracefulness and appropriate splendour of the scene."

His Majesty's visit was a pivotal event. What had previously been considered as the primitive dress of mountain people, now became recognised as the National Dress of Scotland. King George IV had rekindled an interest in tartan and, most importantly of all, he had given the royal seal of approval to the Scottish way of dressing.

The passionate commitment of Sir Walter Scott to the heritage and the value of tartan to Scotland has been equally shared by the Kinloch Anderson Company for more than 150 years.

The connection is stronger than shared values – there is a family connection.

William Anderson founded the company with two of his sons, William Joseph Kinloch Anderson and Andrew Hislop Anderson. In November 1874 Andrew married Joanna Hope Scott, a direct descendant of Sir Walter Scott.

Sir Walter Scott is particularly relevant to the Kinloch Anderson story for a third reason. William Eric Kinloch Anderson KT FRSE, brother of Douglas Kinloch Anderson, fifth generation, is renowned for his work as an authority on Sir Walter Scott and the editing author of the *Journals of Sir Walter Scott*. Sir Eric was also a director of the Abbotsford Trust which restored Scott's beautiful home in the Scottish Borders and which is open to the public.

Sir Walter Scott and the Scott Monument

The death of Sir Walter Scott was announced in 1832 and it was resolved to raise a monument in his memory. The foundation stone of the Scott Monument was laid on August 15, 1840, but it was not until August 17, 1846 that the monument was completed and formally inaugurated by the Lord Provost the Right Honourable Adam Black.

The Scott Monument is Edinburgh's grandest ornament and is one of the finest Gothic monumental edifices in the world. It rises to a height of 200 feet 6 inches (61.11 metres) and there is a spiral staircase of 287 steps reaching to the top, from where there is a magnificent view. From the base platform there are four pillars connected by four pointed arches, the whole forming a lofty canopy over a statue of the man himself. The pilasters (rectangular columns) are crowned with ornamental likenesses of sixteen Scottish poets. The flying buttresses terminate respectively with a carved figure of a jester, a nun, a friar and a Knight Templar. There are four galleries in the building, each gorgeously decorated.

The statue of Scott is in Carrara marble and shows him with his favourite dog "Maida" by his side. There are sixty-four statuettes in the niches around the monument which represent the various characters of Scott's work.

Above: Sir Walter Scott, (1771–1832). In 1822 Scott created a spectacular pageant in honour of King George IV. This event gave the royal seal of approval to the Scots way of dressing – and Highland Dress has never looked back.

Left: The statue of Scott at the base of the monument, where Scott is depicted with his beloved dog Maida.

Overleaf: The Scott Monument pictured in 1868.

Introduction
NORTH BRIDGE, EDINBURGH

WHERE IT ALL BEGAN

KINLOCH ANDERSON
DRESS TARTAN

T HE Kinloch Anderson story of six generations has its roots in Edinburgh, and their story as tailors and outfitters began on the city's North Bridge. The number of records of tailors and clothiers of the day, with addresses of North Bridge and South Bridge, shows that this was Edinburgh's centre for tailoring in the 1860s – the garment district.

The Handbook To Edinburgh for use of the passengers on board the Anchor Line of Steamers declares:

> *The North Bridge, which runs straight south, was built in 1767–1772, at a cost of £18,000. It consists of three great central arches, two small open side arches and a number of small vault arches at the ends. The span of each of the great arches is 72 feet; and the height, from the ground to the top of the parapet of the centre arches, is 68 feet. The entire length, from Princes Street to the High Street, is 1125 feet. The average daily number of foot passengers traversing the bridge is said to be upwards of 90,000 – the number of carriages and other vehicles, upwards of 2000. The view eastwards and westwards from the centre of the bridge, in a clear day, is very attractive.*

As remains true for today's retail environment, location for footfall was key and William Anderson clearly had an eye for where "passing trade" could be found.

Page 21 and swatch above: Dress tartans frequently change a clan tartan colour in the design to white or a light colour and this makes them quite distinctive. The Kinloch Anderson Dress tartan is based on the original Kinloch Anderson tartan, with the predominance of cream replacing the green.

Opposite: The premises of North Bridge Street in the mid-nineteenth century, from the Lithograph by Samuel Dunkinfield Swarbreck, 1837. The entrance to the premises, No. 62, to be occupied by Gorrie & Anderson some years later, is conveniently marked by the gentleman's raised hat.

In the illustration:
55 J. Anderson jun., Bookseller
56 Jas. Howden and Co., Jewellers
57 Benjamin Burk's Tavern
58 Franklin Bros, Jewellers
59 Romanes & Paterson, Silkmercers
60 Mrs Maclellan, Bookbinder
61 Jacob Ashenheim, Jeweller
62 Wm. Marshall, Goldsmith
63 Wm. Donaldson, Clothier
63 John Harvey's Royal Bazaar
64 P. Mackay and Son, Hatters
65 Albion Cloth Company

Right: The shops and offices of North Bridge, 1885.

Right: This 1863 map shows the location of North Bridge Street at right angles to Princes Street and Waterloo Place, with the position of No. 62 indicated by a red circle.

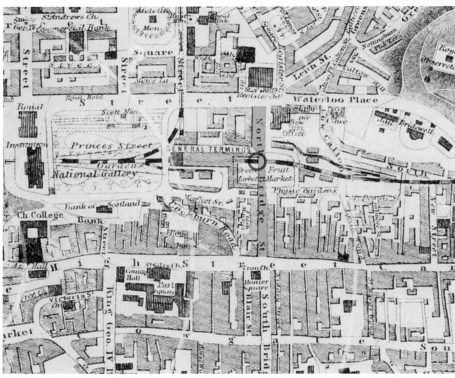

Much has been written about the North Bridge, that important engineering work, spanning the valley that separated the Old and the New Town. It was among the first of the great undertakings upon which the City of Edinburgh embarked.

The North Bridge was built to connect the Old Town of Edinburgh with the fields on the opposite, north side of the valley, soon to be covered with the handsome streets and houses of the entrepreneurial development plans for the New Town. It was also logical that improved access was desired towards the south, and the South Bridge of the present day continues to be one of the most important business thoroughfares of the city.

Revolutionary ideas poured in through the gap of the North Bridge. Beside the north-eastern corner of the bridge, on the spot later occupied by the General Post Office, rose the first regularly licensed theatre in the Scottish capital: the old Theatre Royal. Close by, the slopes of Moultries Hill is where open-air preachings were held. The top of Moultries Hill is where St James Square was later built. Thousands came to listen to evangelists whose missions brought about the religious revival known as the "Great Awakening".

Not without some adventure, would a journey be made across the bridge after dark. The North Bridge had been built with unpaved and unlit connecting streets. Linkboys – boys who carried a flaming torch to light your way – were common in those days before street lighting. The linkboy's fee was usually one farthing and his torch was made from burning pitch and tow.

Now, as then, passengers on the North Bridge still have fantastic views. The Castle Rock and the solid mass of the Old Town buildings – "Auld Reekie" itself – is ragged with spires and chimney-tops between the smoky grey of its base colour with the darker closes in between and the high relief of its many storeyed gables. This majestic skyline runs from the castle battlements down the long slope towards Holyrood. Rising in a sheer cliff above the roofs of the Canongate, the Salisbury Crags shine in the sunlight or hang black and threatening in foul weather, and behind them lies the peak of an extinct volcano, Arthur's Seat.

However, in the early days, the outlook from the North Bridge was more spacious and unobstructed than it is today. Looking eastward from the parapet of the bridge, you could see North Berwick Law, the Bass Rock, the sandhills of Gullane, the waters of the Firth of Forth and, to the north, even glimpses of Fife.

It was half a century later that the buildings on the west side of the bridge, at the northern end, came into existence. These were where Gorrie & Anderson, William Anderson's first business enterprise, were to be found at 62 New Buildings. Their construction raised strong protest from the citizens of the day who complained that the block closed out the much-admired view of the castle with the valley beneath. Today, a great former railway hotel, the

Above: Edinburgh's Waverley Station pictured in the 1890s.

Balmoral occupies this site – another structure that originally encountered objections on the grounds that its bulk and height dwarfed the surrounding buildings and hampered the view from the North Bridge.

The world below the bridge has seen great changes since the arches first bridged the valley. Foundries, breweries, Trinity College Church with its adjoining hospital and college, the first orphan hospital, the original Lady Glenorchy's Chapel and the old Physic Gardens were among the earliest of the many developments that were lost by the change that has swept through the valley. The gardens were the first to be planted in Scotland for the promotion of the study of botany on ground that had been in part recovered from the Nor Loch. Due to flooding, botany had ultimately to move and seek other quarters for its herbs and flowers in Leith Walk and then finally to Inverleith Park where the Botanic Gardens remain to this day.

The coming of the railway was perhaps the greatest change of all. Journeys that used to take days would now take mere hours, opening up Edinburgh to new trade and tourism.

All of these events and landmarks set the scene for the Kinloch Anderson story.

Chapter One
WILLIAM ANDERSON

FIRST GENERATION

KINLOCH ANDERSON
HUNTING TARTAN

WILLIAM Anderson, founder of the present-day Kinloch Anderson Company, was born in Cranston, Midlothian in Scotland on August 2, 1818 – 200 years before the date on which the company that he founded would celebrate its 150th anniversary. William married Mary Hislop in Stow, Midlothian in 1841. William Joseph Kinloch Anderson was their first child, born in Govan in Glasgow on January 5, 1846. Their second child, Andrew Hislop Anderson was born in 1849.

Records show that William Hislop Anderson first learnt his trade with the firm John Rae, a clothier and hatter in Queen Street, Glasgow. Later in his career he returned to the east of Scotland to work at Marshall & Aitken, 27 North Bridge, Edinburgh, where he worked as principal cutter.

On December 17, 1860, William set up his business at 62 New Buildings, North Bridge, Edinburgh in partnership with Thomas Stoddart.

Two years later, Thomas Stoddart left and so William Anderson formed a new partnership with William Gorrie who had also been an employee at Marshall & Aitken.

Gorrie & Anderson

Advertisements were placed in *The Edinburgh Evening Courant* and *The Witness* to announce the beginnings of Gorrie & Anderson. In this clipping from *The Edinburgh Evening Courant* – Wednesday April 23, 1862, we read:

> *On 23rd April 1862 William Gorrie begs respectfully to announce that, having left the Establishment of Messrs. Marshall & Aitken,*

Page 27 and swatch above: In Victorian times, hunting tartans were worn for hunting and shooting. The Kinloch Anderson Hunting tartan reflects this characteristic with varied shades of green and muted blue. Burgundy maintains a link to the Kinloch Anderson tartan and black and gold represent the Kinloch Anderson Company logo.

Opposite: William Anderson, founder of the present-day Kinloch Anderson Company.

Right: This photograph, by JCH Balmain, shows a view looking to the south across the old, narrower North Bridge from beside the bronze statue of the Duke of Wellington outside Register House at the East End of Princes Street.

© The Yerbury family

Above, and right: Gorrie & Anderson were at 62 North Bridge. (The numbering on the right hand side [west side] was 62, 63, 64, 65.)
North Bridge was formerly known as North Bridge Street.

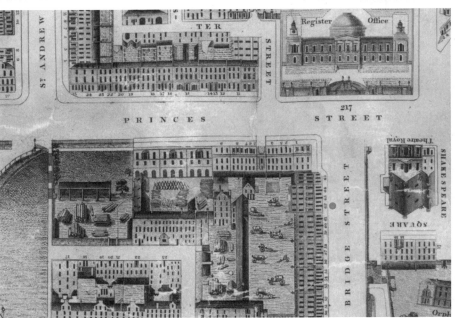

Clothiers, where he has been for nearly eighteen years, he has now commenced business at New Buildings, North Bridge in company with Mr Wm Anderson who was for several years Principal Cutter to the above firm. From Mr Anderson's experience and ability as a Cutter, and by supplying all goods of a superior quality and style at charges more than usually moderate, Gorrie & Anderson have every confidence in soliciting a share of public patronage and support. 62 New Buildings, North Bridge.

Regular advertisements for Gorrie & Anderson appeared in 1862, and for the next few years, which show that their gentlemen's tailoring range also included some tartan garments. Their range of clothing was varied, catering for schoolboys, travelling gentlemen and the clergy. As is still the case now, durability and affordability were of paramount importance. School uniforms of "untearable tweeds" must have proved very useful!

BOYS' DRESS
SAC JACKET SUITS, KNICKERBOCKER SUITS, KILT SUITS
Every style of Boys' dress made up with taste and economy.
**BOYS'
SCHOOL SUITS**
of
UNTEARABLE TWEEDS
EXTREMELY DURABLE, AND VERY MODERATE IN PRICE.

GENTLEMAN'S DRESS
GENTLEMEN'S CLOTHING OF SUPERIOR QUALITY AND
STYLE AT PRICES LOWER THAN ARE USUALLY CHARGED.

**GENTLEMAN'S TWEED SUITS
GORRIE & ANDERSON**
HAVE RECEIVED SEVERAL NEW RARE MIXTURES IN
SCOTCH TWEEDS, OF AN ELASTIC, DURABLE MAKE WHICH
THEY CAN WITH CONFIDENCE RECOMMEND.
Price 63s.
Made up in a Superior Style.

Excursion Suits – Excursion or travelling suits
of Scotch Tweeds.

MADE UP IN A SUPERIOR STYLE,

ON VERY MODERATE TERMS.

To CLERGYMEN
Gorrie & Anderson respectfully inform Clergymen that the Suits supplied
by them can be confidently recommended as being of superior quality
and style, while their prices are lower than usually charged.

Above: Mr William Kinloch Anderson (1874–1949), of the third generation of the company (*see* page 61), was a member of the Queen's (Edinburgh) Rifle Volunteer Brigade and is pictured wearing his 2nd Lieutenant's uniform in 1895.

The Volunteers

The establishment of the volunteer movement in Great Britain was sanctioned on May 12, 1859. As gentleman tailors and military outfitters, Gorrie & Anderson were committed to producing uniforms for this movement and an advertisement in the *Caledonian Mercury*, Saturday July 18, 1863 verifies this.

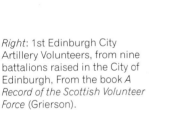

E.R.V.
THE NEW REGULATION UNIFORM
Supplied by
GORRIE & ANDERSON
62 NEW BUILDINGS
NORTH BRIDGE

The ERV were the Edinburgh Rifle Volunteers, just one part of the volunteer movement that was to sweep the country.

In 1859 there was growing tension in Europe and unease in Britain at the strength of the French army, the most powerful military machine in Europe

Right: 1st Edinburgh City Artillery Volunteers, from nine battalions raised in the City of Edinburgh, From the book *A Record of the Scottish Volunteer Force* (Grierson).

GUNNER (in Forage Cap)   GUNNER
1st EDINBURGH A.V.   1st EDINBURGH R.G.A. (V.)
1866   1907
1st EDINBURGH (CITY) R.G.A. (V.)

GUNNER   SERJEANT
1st MIDLOTHIAN A.V.   1st MIDLOTHIAN R.G.A. (V.)
1860   1905
1st MIDLOTHIAN R.G.A. (V.)

WILLIAM ANDERSON'S
FORMATIVE YEARS

1818
▶ The beginning of the Union Canal to connect Edinburgh and Glasgow by water. Estimated cost £240,468, 17s, 2d.

▶ The Honours of Scotland are discovered in a chest in Edinburgh Castle. (Following the Act of Union, they were hidden, walled up in the Crown room of the Castle.) The future George IV, the Prince Regent, authorises Sir Walter Scott to break down the wall, finding the Crown Sceptre, the Sword of State and the Lord Treasurer's Silver Rod of Office.

1820
▶ The "Radical War" of 1820. A slump followed the end of Napoleonic wars in 1815. Unemployment was high. There was great hardship. In 1820 a band of weavers demonstrated against employers' refusals to allow a union, and against high food prices. In Bonnymuir armed forces were sent to counter the demonstrators. Three men were hanged and nineteen deported. Though the protests did not go away, the authorities reacted violently to any dissent.

1821
▶ Steam-packets are introduced between Leith and London. The journey takes sixteen hours. The largest steam vessel is called *The City of Edinburgh* and has beds for 100 people.

at the time. Following the war in the Crimea, the British army had been reduced from over 230,000 to under 100,000. Of those remaining, many were unfit for combat.

In 1813 Britain had been threatened by France and had experienced a shortage of manpower in the armed forces, and so Parliament had introduced a Militia Bill to allow volunteers to serve in Europe. The Militia Bill had been revived in 1852. Units were raised and filled by voluntary enlistment, but also, at that time, conscription if counties failed to meet their quotas. It was intended to be seen as an alternative to the army.

The volunteer force in Great Britain was national, and all ranks and classes took part. By the end of 1859, across the country there were sixteen corps of artillery volunteers with seventy-three batteries, and 330 companies of rifle volunteers. In Scotland there were ten batteries, one subdivision of artillery, forty-nine corps with sixty-seven companies and one subdivision of rifles.

At the outset of this movement in 1859, the volunteer members provided their own arms and equipment and paid for all their own expenses attending the corps, except in the event of its being assembled for actual service. "Uniforms should be as simple as possible, and those of the different companies in each county should be similar."

The uniforms of the earliest volunteer riflemen were uncontrolled. The government, however, then brought in guidelines. For rifle volunteers they were brownish grey with peg-top trousers made to be worn with a tunic, piped with the regimental colour and ornamented with an Austrian knot on the sleeve (pictured right), a low cap of the same cloth with a peak, brown leather belts and a long cape with hood. For artillery the pattern recommended was the same, but of blue cloth with scarlet piping and black belts.

In the company newsletter of July 1972, WJ Kinloch Anderson, referred to the company's history in tailoring for the Volunteers. "Before long, after the death of their father, the two brothers were running the business. Because they were keenly interested in the Volunteers – predecessors of the Territorial Army – they made uniforms for many friends and colleagues and soon built up an enviable reputation in this specialised field. It also included the making of kilts and other tartan garments in which, too, they became acknowledged experts."

Below: This uniform is in the Kinloch Anderson Heritage Museum in Leith. The jacket is shown here, with an illustration of the distinctive Austrian knot ornamentation on the sleeve below.

1823 ▶ The most disastrous fire recorded in Edinburgh breaks out in the High Street and becomes known as "The Great Conflagration". As a consequence of the fire, nearly 400 families are rendered homeless and eight people die.

▶ The Foundation Stone of the Edinburgh Academy is laid, and Sir Walter Scott is listed amongst the first of the directors.

▶ The Royal Botanic Gardens in Leith Walk moves to its present location at Inverleith Row.

1827 ▶ The discovery of the Burke and Hare murders. Burke is executed in 1828.

1831 ▶ The Second Cholera Pandemic reaches Great Britain. Cities such as Newcastle, London, Edinburgh and Glasgow are ravaged by the outbreak. As a result of the outbreak, the intravenous saline drip is developed from the work of Dr Thomas Latta of Leith (1796–1833).

Above: A Princes Street scene from around the time that Gorrie & Anderson were battling the consequences of a strike of journeymen tailors.

The 1866 Strike of the Journeymen Tailors

In the year 1866 there was strike action from many professions. There was economic strife following the Crimean War and workers experienced plummeting wages. The tailors' strike lasted months and their employers, in some cases, sought foreign workers to take their places. In London, Karl Marx's International Workingmen's Association intervened by placing adverts in newspapers in France, Belgium and Switzerland urging tailors of those countries not to take jobs in Britain. Some foreign tailors actually sent money to British strikers.

The Edinburgh Evening Courant – Wednesday April 4, 1866 – reported that at a meeting of the Master Tailors' Association of Edinburgh (the list included Gorrie & Anderson) it was resolved that,

> *"terms be made with the Society of Journeymen who are out on strike and secure a permanent settlement – the undersigned Master Tailors respectfully request the kind forebearance of their customers with regard to orders until arrangements are made which will enable them to resume business."*

WILLIAM ANDERSON'S
FORMATIVE YEARS

1837

▶ King William IV dies. His niece Victoria (1819–1901) becomes Queen of Great Britain, at the age of eighteen.

1842

▶ On February 21, 1842, the Edinburgh to Glasgow railway line was opened.
The first steam railway in Scotland was developed in 1817, but it was not till 1831 that enough progress had been made to claim that an effective steam railway existed. By 1850 it was possible to travel from Aberdeen to London by rail.

1845

▶ From 1845–1851 a severe potato blight created a period of mass starvation in Ireland known as the Great Famine. It was amongst the greatest losses of life in nineteenth-century Europe with deaths estimated at a million. At least a million people are thought to have emigrated as a result of the famine.

▶ The Scottish Highlands are also badly affected by the potato famine for ten years.

A warning from Karl Marx, 1866

A plea to German workers not to take the jobs of Scottish journeymen tailors, was made on behalf of the Central Council of the International Working-men's Association, by Karl Marx, London, May 4, 1866:

Some time ago the London journeymen tailors formed a general association to uphold their demands against the London master tailors. It was a question not only of bringing wages into line with the increased prices of means of subsistence, but also of putting an end to the exceedingly harsh treatment of the workers in this branch of industry. The masters sought to frustrate this plan by recruiting journeymen tailors, chiefly in Belgium, France and Switzerland.

Thereupon the secretaries of the Central Council of the International Workingmen's Association published in Belgian, French and Swiss newspapers a warning which was a complete success.

The London masters were foiled; they had to surrender and meet their workers' just demands.

Defeated in England, the masters are now trying to take counter-measures, starting in Scotland.

The fact is that, as a result of the London events, they had to agree, initially, to a fifteen per cent wage rise in Edinburgh as well.

But secretly they sent agents to Germany to recruit journeymen tailors, particularly in the Hanover and Mecklenburg areas, for importation to Edinburgh. The first group has already been shipped off.

If the Edinburgh masters succeeded, through the import of German labour, in nullifying the concessions they had already made, it would inevitably lead to repercussions in England.

No one would suffer more than the German workers themselves, who constitute in Great Britain a larger number than the workers of all the other Continental nations. And the newly-imported workers, being completely helpless in a strange land, would soon sink to the level of pariahs.

Furthermore, it is a point of honour with the German workers to prove to other countries that they, like their brothers in France, Belgium and Switzerland, know how to defend the common interests of their class and will not become obedient mercenaries of capital in its struggle against labour.

1854

▶ The Crimean War (1854–1856) begins. It is fought by an alliance of Britain, France, Turkey and Sardinia against Russia. Troops suffer from hardship and army maladministration. Florence Nightingale (1820–1910) comes to prominence as a trainer of nurses.

▶ The Third Cholera Pandemic is at its peak. 23,000 deaths occur in Great Britain.

1856

▶ The building of Balmoral Castle is completed. It was purchased privately by Prince Albert in 1852.

1859

▶ On May 12, 1859, the establishment of the volunteer force in Great Britain is sanctioned.

1866

▶ Karl Marx (1818–1883) makes a plea to German workers not to take the jobs of Scottish journeymen tailors who are striking for better conditions and pay.

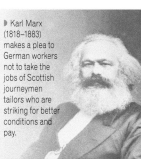

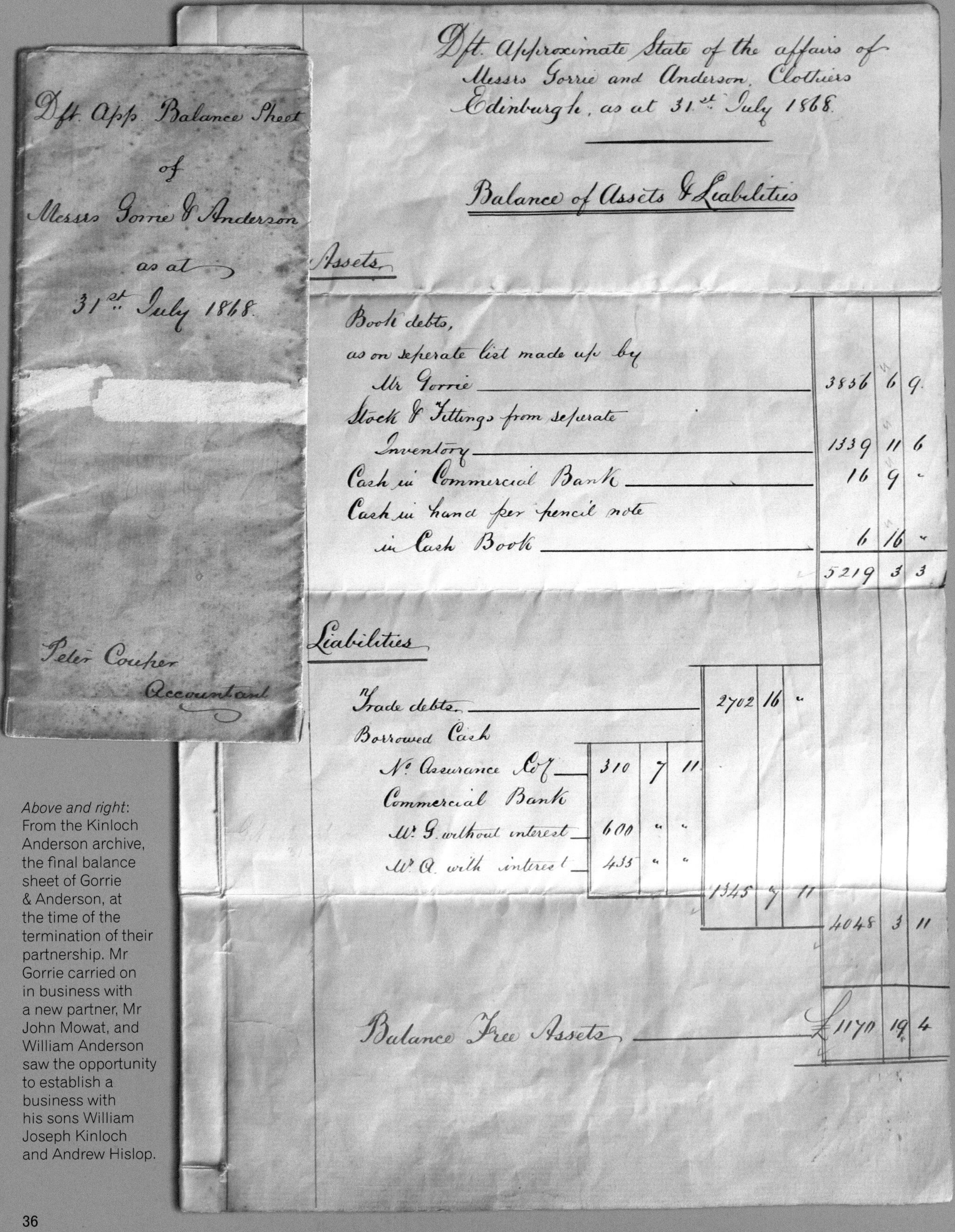

Dft App Balance Sheet

of

Messrs Gorrie & Anderson

as at

31st July 1868

Peter Coucher
Accountant

Dft. Approximate State of the affairs of
Messrs Gorrie and Anderson, Clothiers
Edinburgh, as at 31st July 1868.

Balance of Assets & Liabilities

Assets

Book debts, as on seperate list made up by Mr Gorrie		3856	6 9
Stock & Fittings from seperate Inventory		1339	11 6
Cash in Commercial Bank		16	9 "
Cash in hand per pencil note in Cash Book		6	16 "
		5219	3 3

Liabilities

Trade debts		2702	16 "
Borrowed Cash			
No Assurance Coy	310 7 11		
Commercial Bank			
Mr G without interest	600 " "		
Mr A with interest	435 " "	1345	7 11
		4048	3 11

Balance Free Assets — £1170 19 4

Above and right: From the Kinloch Anderson archive, the final balance sheet of Gorrie & Anderson, at the time of the termination of their partnership. Mr Gorrie carried on in business with a new partner, Mr John Mowat, and William Anderson saw the opportunity to establish a business with his sons William Joseph Kinloch and Andrew Hislop.

Agreement between William Anderson Tailor and Clothier, residing at Number Eight Wharton Place Edinburgh, William Joseph Kinloch Anderson and Andrew Hislop Anderson both Sons of the said William Anderson, and residing with him at Number Eight Wharton Place aforesaid.

First. The said Parties agree to carry on a joint trade and business in Edinburgh as Tailors and Clothiers, in the shop Number fifteen George Street Edinburgh presently occupied by them, under the Copartnery firm of "William Anderson and Sons" and that for the space of Ten years, from and after the first day of August, Eighteen hundred and Sixty eight which notwithstanding the date hereof is hereby declared to have been the commencement of said copartnery. The Lease of the premises to be in name of the firm. –

Second. The Capital Stock of the said copartnery shall consist of Eight hundred Pounds Sterling which shall be contributed by the said William Anderson, and he shall be deemed a Creditor of the Company to the extent of said sum. –

Third. All Bonds, Bills, Contracts, Accounts and other writings relating to the said Trade shall be taken and given under the foresaid Firm and designation of "William Anderson and Sons" and either of the Partners so subscribing in matters relating to the Company Trade shall bind the Company, but no deed whatever that is not so subscribed, shall bind the Company. –

Fourth. The said parties shall keep or cause to be kept, regular and distinct Books containing all the affairs and transactions of the said joint trade, and they shall post and bring forward or cause to be posted and brought forward the Books of the Company from time to time; and also keep a Copy of all important letters relating to the affairs of the Company, and the Company's Books shall be brought to a balance at least once every twelve months as at Thirty first July, and balance Sheets shall be made up in each year, and signed by the said Partners, which shall be examined and attested as correct by Mr James Knox, Accountant in Edinburgh or such other party as may be appointed if wished by either of the partners and then the profit or loss arising from the said Trade shall be divided among or borne by the partners, in the following proportions videlicet, One half to the said William Anderson One fourth to the said William Joseph Kinloch Anderson, and the remaining One fourth to the said Andrew Hislop Anderson

Fifth. At the expiry of this agreement, the Books of the Company shall be brought to a balance, their goods inventoried and a full and complete State of their affairs made up and docqueted by the said Partners; the goods belonging to the Company shall then with all convenient speed be converted into cash, and the debts due to the Company in like manner levied and recovered, the proceeds thereof in the first place to be applied for extinguishing the debts due by the Company, and the residue, if any shall be divided between the said

William Anderson

Wm J K Anderson

A H Anderson

Left: The original partnership agreement between William Anderson and his two sons William Joseph Kinloch and Andrew Hislop, signed November 23, 1868.

George Street

John Geddie in *Romantic Edinburgh* wrote:

"George Street would be the pride and centre of life of Edinburgh New Town if there were no Princes Street. Even as it is, George Street may challenge comparison with its more famous rival on many points of situation, architecture, and history. It can look down from its higher site upon the Princes Street throng, and out and away to the green country, the sea, and the hills. It has its monuments and architectural ornaments; its vistas closed by the two magnificent open spaces, each in its own way almost unrivalled, of St Andrew and Charlotte Squares – on the one hand the lofty pillar of the Melville column and the needle-like spire of St Andrew's Church; on the other the fine dome of St George's."

George Street is half a mile long and 115 feet broad, and was originally a residential quarter, but is now almost entirely occupied by shops. St Andrew Square was built in 1772, and was the first square built in the New Town. Statues and monumental groups preside over its squares and guard its crossways: George IV, William Pitt (1759–1806), Dr Thomas Chalmers (1780–1847).

Every other door has its association with some name or event of note in the social life or literature of the time. The Assembly Rooms and Music Hall were situated in George Street.

From an airy "poet's lodging" behind the Royal Bank, in St James' Square, Sylvander (Robert Burns) spied his Clarinda (Agnes McLehose).

William Creech, publisher of Burns's Edinburgh Edition, had his residence in No. 5 George Street.

Sir Walter Scott has many connections with the street. His widowed mother lived and died in 75 George Street. In No. 108 he took lodgings and brought home his newly-wedded wife. No. 86 was the home of his friend Sir William Forbes, the banker, whose marriage to Scott's "first love", Miss Belches Stuart, nearly broke Scott's heart. No. 39 Castle Street – just a few yards below the corner of George Street – was Scott's home in town where he lived and worked for twenty-eight years. The house next to the Royal Bank in St Andrew Square was long occupied as Douglas's Hotel. It was here that Sir Walter Scott spent the last days he was ever to pass in Edinburgh, after his return from Italy, and just before he went home to Abbotsford to die.

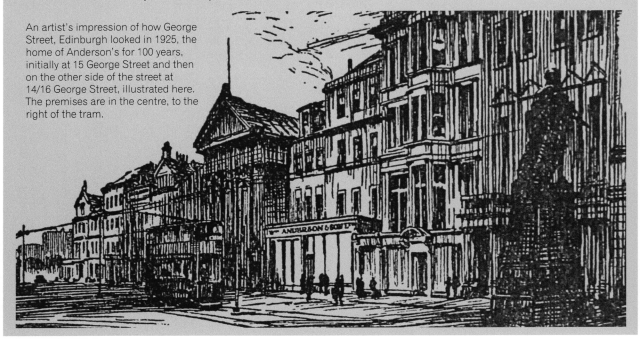

An artist's impression of how George Street, Edinburgh looked in 1925, the home of Anderson's for 100 years, initially at 15 George Street and then on the other side of the street at 14/16 George Street, illustrated here. The premises are in the centre, to the right of the tram.

William Anderson & Sons, Tailors and Clothiers
From *The Edinburgh Gazette*, September 22, 1868:

> *The Co-partnery of Gorrie & Anderson was dissolved by mutual consent on August 1, 1868.*
>
> *In reference to the above, Mr Gorrie begs to intimate that he has assumed a Partner Mr John Mouat, of Andrew Street and continues to carry on the business in all its branches in the same premises formerly, under the designation of Gorrie & Mouat, and trusts to be still favoured with the patronage so liberally bestowed the late firm, 62 New Buildings, North Bridge.*

And so Gorrie & Anderson was no more and William Anderson saw an opportunity to establish his own business with his sons William Joseph Anderson and Andrew Hislop Anderson.

William Anderson set up William Anderson & Sons at 15 George Street. In *The Edinburgh Evening Courant* – Tuesday November 9, 1869. The inclusion of a "card" was an "announcement".

WM ANDERSON & SONS, TAILORS AND CLOTHIERS
15 GEORGE STREET (OPPOSITE COMMERCIAL BANK) EDINBURGH.
The Cutting Department under the Superintendence of Mr A., Sen.,
of the late firm of Gorrie Anderson, North Bridge.

And with that "card" a new chapter in the Kinloch Anderson story began.

William Anderson and his wife Mary Hislop had six children: Eliza, William Joseph, Andrew Hislop, Robert Walter, Mary Jane and Zerub Baillie.

William Anderson was fifty years of age when he founded the company with his two sons William Joseph, aged twenty-two, and Andrew Hislop, aged twenty.

The date of the company's move from North Bridge to 15 George Street is, from the "card", some time before November 9, 1869 but after September 1868, with the partnership agreement being signed on November 23, 1868.

The new business built upon the old, and the military tailoring continued to grow in significance. From the early tailoring of uniforms for the Edinburgh Rifle Volunteers, William Anderson & Sons' business in George Street had grown substantially:

In *The Scotsman* Tuesday April 11, 1871, an advertisement read:

UNIFORMS
MILITIA AND VOLUNTEER
YEOMANRY ETC
STRICT REGULATION – PRICES MODERATE
William Anderson & Sons
Clothiers and Military Outfitters
– BY APPOINTMENT –
TAILORS TO CITY OF EDINBURGH AND MIDLOTHIAN COAST ARTILLERY VOLUNTEERS

As bespoke Scottish tailors, William Anderson & Sons made kilts and Highland Dress clothing items. Customers joined the forces and if they then became officers, they had to be responsible for acquiring their own uniform. The saying "it is well known that the last person to be paid was the tailor" probably stems from this time, indicating that officers received no uniform allowance from their regiment. Anderson's would have frequently been chosen because they could provide so many different uniforms, but there was plenty of competition from many tailors making bespoke garments in those days.

William Anderson had only worked for three years with his two sons when he died in 1871. Little would he have thought that he had launched a business that was to become a renowned Scottish clothing company over six generations.

Right: Deputy-Lieutenant and Vice-Lieutenant uniforms.

Chapter Two
WILLIAM JOSEPH KINLOCH ANDERSON and ANDREW HISLOP ANDERSON

SECOND GENERATION

KINLOCH ANDERSON BLACK
AND WHITE TARTAN

WILLIAM Joseph Kinloch Anderson (1846–1901) and Andrew Hislop Anderson (1849–1902) inherited the senior management of the business from their father. Together the brothers helped establish the success of the company and create a profitable legacy for future generations of their family.

Andrew Hislop Anderson (1849–1902)

On November 13, 1874, Andrew Hislop Anderson married Joanna Hope Scott, a direct descendant of Sir Walter Scott. Andrew and Joanna had twelve children: William, Elizabeth, Mary, Ethel, Georgina, Joanna, Andrew, Beatrice, Walter, Jessie, Herbert and Evelyne.

Around this time there was the period of economic depression known as the "Panic of 1873". In Britain it resulted in bankruptcies, escalating unemployment, a halt in public spending and a major trade slump that lasted until 1897. The years from 1873 to 1896 are sometimes also referred to as the "Long Depression", and most European countries experienced a drastic fall in prices. Hard times for many, but some corporations were able to work with this, reduce production costs and achieve better productivity rates. During this period, despite these incredibly challenging times, William Anderson & Sons were not only surviving but they were doing well.

Kathleen Elizabeth Glover, great granddaughter of Andrew Hislop Anderson, wrote: "the William Kinloch Andersons have always been

Page 41 and swatch above: The black and white colours of the Kinloch Anderson Black and White tartan are universally popular and distinctive. In Scotland these colours are familiar to us in names such as the Black Grouse, the Black Isle, the White Loch and of course the black and white puffins which can be found along our shores.

Opposite: William Joseph Kinloch Anderson (left) and his brother Andrew Hislop Anderson (right).

Above: Andrew Hislop Anderson and his wife Joanna with their family in 1897.

They had twelve children: William (21), Elizabeth (20), Mary (19), Joanna (18), Georgina (16), Ethel (14), Evelyne (12), Andrew (11), Beatrice (10), Walter (9), Jessie (7), and Herbert (5). One of their daughters is missing from the picture.

Portrait taken by the James Patrick Photographic Studios, 52 Comiston Road, Edinburgh.

involved in the management of the firm, while the Hislop Andersons were responsible for the tailoring," and the company archives substantiate this division of responsibilities. Andrew Hislop Anderson's role would most likely have involved the day-to-day management of staff in the shop and the workshop.

In a speech given in 1925 by his nephew, third generation director William Kinloch Anderson, at a celebration in honour of long-serving employees, we learn that in the premises in George Street around the year 1890 they had, he estimated, twenty-four employees – six in the shop and eighteen in the basement workshop. Only one machinist was a woman (a Miss Reid) and all the rest were men. William also describes the working conditions. The day started at 6 am and they did not close till 6 or 7 pm. He observes that the advances of the 1920s such as "gas stoves, electric irons, pressing machines, surging and button-holing machines had not then been thought of." The workshop of 1890 was a darker more cramped place in comparison to the third generation's well-lit and comfortable workplace in 1925.

The Long Depression

The Long Depression was a worldwide economic recession, beginning in 1873 and running to 1879 – even till 1896 in some parts of the world. It was the most severe in Europe and the United States. Though a period of general deflation and a general contraction, it did not have the severe economic retrogression of the Great Depression. The ledger below shows that in the sales period during the Long Depression, William Anderson & Sons were steadily increasing their sales.

Below and right: A sales ledger showing the sales period during the challenging times of the "Long Depression".

A notebook cover with handwritten label: "Totals of Sales from 1869"

Note (vertical, left of table): Business started at 15 George Street Edinburgh on 20 August 1866 H.N.G.

	1869			1870			1871			1872			1873			1874			1875			1876		
January				164	9	4½	184	13	10	222	10		228	19	6	236	10	10	246	15	.	219	12	5
February				188	14	4	294	3	8	202	8	9	286	3	.	305	4	4	451	14	5	318	1	4
March				416	14	5?	624	.	4	431	12	1	448	18	6	525	10	10	638	5	11	450	4	1
April				257	13	9	300	11	1	443	14	8	310	14	4	537	14	2	539	14	6?	592	19	8
May				446	6	6	468	12	4	424	11	9	544	14	6	446	10	.	469	15	.	628	4	11
June				221	.	11	321	.	11	322	19	3	508	9	2?	345	16	3	564	6	11	510	9	.
July	132	12	3	228	.	4	281	2	4?	274	18	9	291	11	.	406	10	4	286	8	8	359	3	9
August	205	13	4	186	9	4	182	11	2	208	-	1	206	1	6?	144	19	10	262	4	8	233	3	.
September	342	6	5	265	1	8	315	15	8	423	2	11	423	1	4	460	11	8.	505	1	1?	514	1	4
October	348	13	8	346	3	3	310	6	1	393	14	4	401	.	.	543	3	.	490	14	10?	435	9	.
November	261	12	11		16	11	302	19	8	21	9	2	340	1	3	351	2	9	391	9	8	421	14	5
December	270	16	9		2	6	210	.	.		.	.	243	11	3	338	2	3½	305	2	4	341	14	.
	1561	15	4	2784	16	10½	3498	14	1½	3342	5	-	4286	8	11	4934	16	9½	5145	2	1½	5024	19	11
	6 months						less 2 months			less 2 months														

45

Above: Horse-drawn bus, c.1900 on the route to Newington and Craigmillar Park, where William Joseph Kinloch Anderson lived at The Elms.

Also speaking at the same event in 1925, employee Mr JJ Bell, who started his working life with the company in 1900, remembered William Joseph and Andrew Hislop fondly.

> "Now, I am not given to flattery, I hate flattery, but I may say that if you had gone over the whole City of Edinburgh you would not have got two gentlemen who were more esteemed, and almost loved, by their fellow men... As regards Mr Andrew Anderson, I do not know how to speak of him. He knew his business from A to Z [cries of hear, hear]. He was a very generous man. I have known customers even today [1925] speak about Mr Andrew Anderson and his kindness."

William Joseph Kinloch Anderson (1846–1901)

William Joseph Kinloch Anderson was the elder of the two brothers and the first of the Anderson family to be given the name of Kinloch. Apparently, his father worked at Falkland for a Mr Kinloch with whom he became very friendly and William was therefore named after him.

William Joseph Kinloch married Mary Wilson in 1873. Mary was one of two sisters from Ballencrieff Farm in East Lothian. When their father died, the farm was sold and they built two adjacent houses in Marmion Road, North Berwick. They and their respective families spent a couple of months there every summer whilst William Joseph Kinloch and his brother-in-law "went up to Edinburgh by train each day to work". This East Lothian summer residence probably explains the picture on the right of William Joseph Kinloch with his family outside the Open Arms at Dirleton.

William Joseph Kinloch and Mary had eleven children, of whom twins died at birth. William was the eldest (who would go on to run the third generation of the company), the others were James W, Robert K, Elizabeth T, Frederick Kinloch, Mary H, Zerub Baillie, Emily F and Walter Kinloch.

Whilst running the growing George Street business, William Joseph Kinloch Anderson found time to make a contribution to the City of Edinburgh. He began public life in Edinburgh as a High

1850 ▶ Foundation Stone of The Scottish National Gallery in Edinburgh is laid. The gallery opens in 1859.

1852 ▶ Duke of Wellington Statue is erected in front of Register House in Edinburgh.

1856 ▶ In the USA, Singer introduces their first home sewing machines, with a popular hire-purchase plan. By 1860, Singer is the largest manufacturer of sewing machines in the world. In the UK, Chadwick & Jones, make home sewing machines at Ashton-under-Lyne.

Constable and he was Moderator of that body when he was chosen in 1885 for the town council as a representative of Newington Ward, where he lived at The Elms, Craigmillar Park. He served this ward and his native city so well that in November 1894, after a membership of nine years, he was unanimously elected to the Magistracy. In 1896, Bailie Kinloch Anderson was re-elected without a contest and was reappointed to the Magistracy on which he served his full term of three years thereafter, or five years in all.

Above: William Joseph Kinloch Anderson with his family outside the Open Arms at Dirleton.

1861
▸ Building of the Industrial Museum – then called the Museum of Science and Art – now the Royal Scottish Museum in Edinburgh.

▸ GPO built at Waterloo Place, Edinburgh – previously the site of the Theatre Royal.

1868
▸ Craigleith Hospital and Poorhouse established in Edinburgh. Now the Western General Hospital.

1870
▸ Construction begins on the Edinburgh Royal Infirmary. It will become Europe's biggest hospital under one roof.

1872
▸ Ross Fountain is built in Edinburgh's Princes Street Gardens.

▸ Restoration of Saint Giles Cathedral begins. (Completed 1883.)

Right: As a councillor, William Joseph Kinloch Anderson became involved in the affairs of the city, including organising the International Exhibition of Industry, Science and Art, 1886, held at the Meadows, Edinburgh.

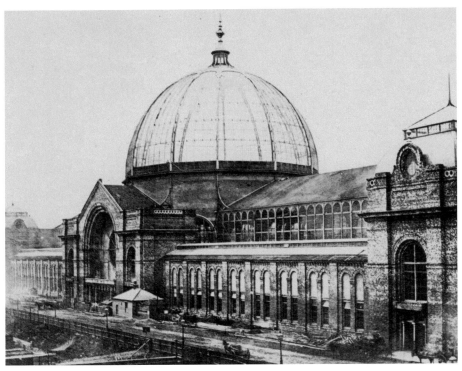

Below: The Gowans sundial in the Meadows, Edinburgh. Its inscription reads: "Erected in commemoration of the opening of the International Exhibition by HRH Prince Albert Victor of Wales on May 6, 1886. | The Most Honourable Marquis Of Lothian K.T. President. | The Right Honourable Thomas Clark. Lord Provost of the City. | James Gowans. Lord Dean Of Guild. Chairman of the Executive Council."

The International Exhibition of Industry, Science and Art, 1886

As a councillor, Bailie Kinloch Anderson became involved in the affairs of the city, which included some of the enormous amount of work required for setting up the International Exhibition of Industry, Science and Art, 1886. Running from May 6 to October 30, it was held at the Meadows, Edinburgh – a sensational spectacle, opened by Prince Albert Victor, grandson of the then reigning British monarch, Queen Victoria.

The Meadows is a familiar feature of Edinburgh today, yet very little now remains to even hint at such a spectacle having been held there. However, the Memorial Pillars at the end of Melville Drive remain and also the sundial designed by James Gowans to the west side of the park.

The architect Sir James Gowans (1821–1890), was largely responsible for organising the 1886 exhibition and was a close colleague of William Joseph Kinloch who would have undoubtedly known about this sundial.

The *Book Of Old Edinburgh* by John Charles Dunlop was published in

EVENTS IN THE TIME OF THE
SECOND GENERATION

1873

▶ The Panic of 1873: A financial crisis that triggered an economic depression in Europe and North America that lasts from 1873 until 1877. In fact the effects are felt even longer in France and Britain.

1875

▶ Alexander Graham Bell (1847–1922) makes the first sound transmission on June 2, 1875. He formed the Bell Telephone Company in 1877.

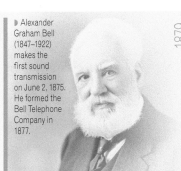

1879

▶ The Tay Bridge collapses in a severe storm and a train carrying around seventy-five people plummets into the River Tay. No one survives.

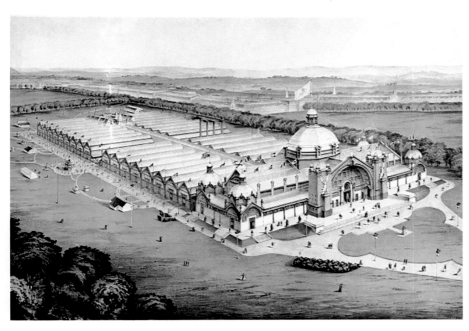

1886 for the International Exhibition. There was an "Old Edinburgh Street exhibit" section where there is an acknowledgement to "Contractors For Old Edinburgh" including:

> **WILLIAM ANDERSON & SONS**
> **MILITARY TAILORS, EDINBURGH (FOR DRESS OF THE OLD TOWN GUARD)**

The International Exhibition of Electricity, Engineering, General Inventions and Industries, 1890

Another great international exhibition was held in Edinburgh just four years later in 1890 – at Meggetland, to the south-west of the city.

The International Exhibition of Electricity, Engineering, General Inventions and Industries was a showcase – a celebration, too, of engineering and the railways – coming just months after the opening of the Forth Bridge.

What a time of great excitement and expectation too. The exhibition was an

1880 ▶ By this time, the Glasgow Fair, with its steamer trips "doon the watter" and train excursions to the Highlands, has become a summer institution.

CLUTHA No12 GLASC

1882 ▶ In the Highlands, just a few families own most of the land. A Highland Land League is formed to resist continuing enclosures of land and eviction of tenants.

1883 ▶ Edinburgh Royal Lyceum Theatre opens with *Much Ado About Nothing* by the company of the London Lyceum Theatre, starring Henry Irving (1838–1905) and Ellen Terry (1847–1928, right).

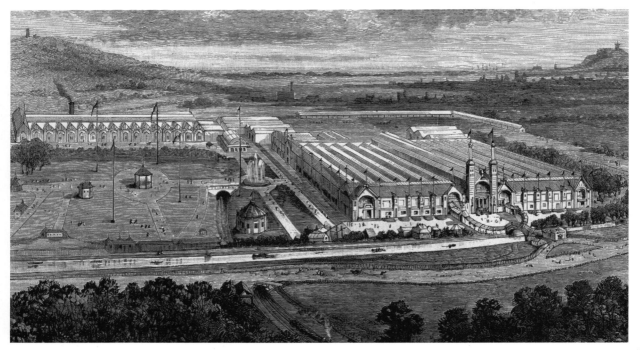

Above: The Edinburgh International Exhibition, 1890.

international spectacle with exhibits from around the world. Technology and invention were capturing the imagination of everyone. People were marvelling at the dawn of electricity and what it could do.

Visiting these exhibitions also gave members of the public a taste of the exotic and a look into the new exciting technologies of the future. Even the temporary buildings in which they were housed were imposing.

Edinburgh also managed to combine the exhibition itself with performance and entertainment. The concerts of music and choral works, arranged throughout the exhibition, were a festival in themselves.

The exhibition drew almost as many visitors through its doors as the 1886 exhibition had done – over two million people, on a site of larger proportions, with transportation connecting sections, including an electric railway, switchback railway and telpherage railway.

Bailie Kinloch Anderson was highly involved. He was a Vice Chairman and a subscriber to the Guarantee Fund relating to the exhibition.

In the category "Outside Exhibits", Exhibit 299D is listed as a "'Sun Dial'. (Nearby 2 x 'Fountains', a 'Japanese Village', a 'Steam Fire Engine Station'

EVENTS IN THE TIME OF THE SECOND GENERATION

1884
▶ The ancient site of Blackford Hill is bought by the Edinburgh Corporation. (The adjacent Hermitage of Braid estate was gifted to the city of Edinburgh in 1938, by John McDougal. The Hermitage is now used as a public park.)

1888
▶ Scottish Labour Party founded. Merges with Independent Labour party in 1895. Scots such as Keir Hardie (1856–1915, right) and Robert Cunninghame-Graham (1852–1936) were prominent in the formative years of the Labour movement.

1889
▶ Elected county councils are introduced.

1890
▶ Opening of the Forth Bridge.

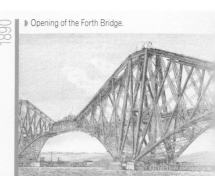

Left: The sundial presented by William Joseph Kinloch Anderson to the City of Edinburgh, situated in Inverleith Park.

The presence of field guns in the photograph suggests that it was taken on Saturday April 15, 1899, on the occasion of the Review of the Edinburgh Garrison, by Lord Wolseley. The total muster was about 250 of the Scots Greys; about 60 of the 29th Company of the Eastern Division Royal Artillery from Leith Fort and about 450 of the 1st Battalion Gordon Highlanders from Edinburgh Castle. The turnout of spectators to view the show was probably the largest which has ever been seen in Inverleith Park – an alternative venue for the Review, as the drill ground at Queen's Park was under repair.

and an exhibit by the 'North British Railway Station')". The sundial was made by Robert Thomson & Sons, monumental sculptors and stone carvers, of Murieston Lane, Dalry Road (located opposite Dalry Cemetery Gate), experts in working with marble, granite and freestone. Their works were a mere one and a half miles from the 1890 Exhibition grounds.

At this time, the City of Edinburgh was actively developing public spaces for communities, and Councillor Kinloch Anderson was prominent in the city's plans, amongst them the creation of Inverleith Park.

He purchased the sundial from the International Exhibition, as a gift to mark the creation of Inverleith Park, perhaps recalling the sundial made for the 1886 Expo by his colleague Sir James Gowans and it became the centre-piece of Inverleith Park's Sundial Garden.

The year 2018 was the Kinloch Anderson Company's 150th Anniversary which was commemorated by the restoration of this sundial, donated to the city by Bailie Kinloch Anderson in 1890. A garden party was held in the Sundial Garden of Inverleith Park in June 2018 and the commemorative Kinloch Anderson 150th Anniversary Sundial tartan was designed.

1892 ▸ Women still don't have the vote but the Scottish universities formally accept women undergraduates. (In 1870 Edinburgh medical students had rioted against women being allowed to attend anatomy lectures.)

1894 ▸ 65,000 Scottish coal miners go on strike for five months, disrupting many other coal-dependent industries.

1896 ▸ Opening of the Glasgow Subway (right).

▸ Edinburgh's first cable car came in 1896 with the Edinburgh Northern Tramway Company. A revolution in public transport was about to begin, it spelled the end of horse-drawn travel. Tramcars gripped onto cables under the streets pulled vehicles along at 8mph. By the 1920s most of Edinburgh was served by electric trams.

1900 ▸ Founding of the Labour Party. Keir Hardie becomes its first leader.

Inverleith Park

This description of Inverleith Park (1914) is from the *City of Edinburgh Report on Public Parks, Gardens and Open Spaces*, by John W McHattie, Superintendent of Parks and Gardens, written nearly twenty-five years after Councillor Kinloch Anderson took part in the official opening ceremony. It reflects the vision that the council, and Councillor Kinloch Anderson particularly, had for Inverleith Park. At 61 acres, it was the fourth-largest in the city, after the Braids, Blackford Hill, Saughtonhall Park and the Meadows. The area had previously been farm lands belonging to Inverleith House (the House itself, with the Arboretum, was acquired by the Royal Botanic Garden in 1877).

Above: John W McHattie, the City of Edinburgh's Superintendent of Parks and Gardens from 1901–23.

The ground, with Farm Buildings, was purchased from Mr Charles Rocheid of Inverleith at a cost of £33,500. Entry to the greater portion of the ground was at Whitsunday 1889. Entry to the remainder – being the Farm Buildings, field to the south thereof and two Roadways – was at Martinmas 1899. The works undertaken were mainly for Roadways, Ride and Drains, planting and laying out Grounds, New Greenhouses, alterations of Farm Buildings and construction of Pavilion, &c. The Expenses connected with the acquisition of the Property were £226 7s 7d, and £12,659 6s 11d has been spent on the works above specified.

This Park has been kept in good condition ... The Hothouses and Nursery are in good order, producing large quantities of plants, trees and shrubs, which are distributed and planted in the different Parks,

Gardens and open spaces in the City. There are two gymnasia, one for boys and one for girls: two Bowling Greens, four Tennis Courts and two Golf Courses; also a Ride for Horse Riding exercise. Football, Cricket and Shinty are permitted, and there is a good Shelter, Ladies' and Gentlemen's Cloakroom and Pavilion for Football and Cricket ... A portion of the Pavilion is used as a Shelter by the old men frequenting the Park. Games, books and magazines are provided and much appreciated.

The Pond has been supplied with fresh water from the water main, so that the weeds, which were for a time a source of trouble and expense, have to a great extent been removed. There is now a fine sheet of clear water which is used for Model Yachting and water fowl.

The gymnasium was used by 180 children per day, May to September, totalling 23,940 children in the year. Play was free on both the eighteen- and nine-hole golf courses, each attracting over 30,000 people a year. There were twenty-eight football pitches, with eighty home clubs, 784 matches and 17,248 players registered for the season. The cricket pitch had four clubs and twenty-nine matches. Rugby football, rounders and skating were also permitted. Music was provided on Friday evenings in June.

Below: Looking across Inverleith Pond towards Edinburgh.

The Death of William Joseph Kinloch Anderson
The Scotsman November 15, 1901

The death took place yesterday, in Edinburgh under circumstances of startling – almost tragic suddenness – of Councillor Kinloch Anderson, one of the most highly respected members of the Town Council.

He never completely recovered from the effects of a serious paralytic seizure which overtook him about eighteen months ago, but the robust constitution which he had enjoyed up until then, and his naturally buoyant disposition, stood him in good stead and he made what was in the circumstances regarded as a good recovery – so good that he was able to return to public life, in which he has taken an active part for about fifteen years. At the general municipal election of last year, he was still laid aside by illness, but such was the esteem that he was held in Newington Ward that he was elected in his absence at the top of the poll. After his return to the Council Chamber his strength seemed gradually to improve, and he was able to attend to his own business and to take a fair share of work at committee as well as Council meetings. Only yesterday forenoon he attended a meeting of the Treasurer's Committee and remarked, in answer to an enquiry by one of the Corporation officials, that he had not felt so well for a long time. He took his departure from the City Chambers about a quarter to twelve to return to his place of business. On the way down The Mound a friend observed him looking very ill. He hailed a cab and took Mr Anderson to George Street, where Mr William Kinloch Anderson, his eldest son, seeing that his father's condition was grave, decided to drive him home to Newington. On the way, however, Mr Anderson became so ill that his son directed the cab to go to the Royal Infirmary. By the time that institution was reached, Councillor Anderson had collapsed and he died a few minutes after removal from the cab.

Above: The Mound, Edinburgh, by the Royal Academy.

Mr Anderson began public life as a High Constable and he was Moderator of that body when he was chosen in 1885 for the Town Council as a representative of Newington Ward, filling the vacancy created by the retirement of Lord Provost Sir George Harrison. He served this ward and his city so well that in November 1894, after a membership of nine years, he was unanimously elected to the Magistracy, along with Bailie Gulland. By the election of Sir Andrew McDonald to the Lord Provostship at the same time, Bailie Kinloch Anderson had to present himself to the electors in 1896, a year earlier than otherwise would have been the case, but he was re-elected without contest and was reappointed to the Magistracy on which he served his full term of three years, or five years in all.

In 1897, during the currency of this term of Bailieship, he was nominated for the Lord Provostship along with Sir Mitchell Thomson and Treasurer McCrae, but failed to get the necessary support for the civic chair, and it was generally understood that the worry of that contest upon a somewhat nervous disposition did his health no good. On retiring from the Bailieship he was appointed a Judge of Police. In the general administration of the city's affairs, Mr Anderson took an active and worthy part but perhaps his most valuable work for the community was that which he rendered as convener of the Works Committee of the Edinburgh and Leith Gas Commission. He showed a wonderful grasp of all the details of the Gas Commission's business; he was always able to make his monthly statements interesting, and to him belongs much of the credit for carrying through the large scheme for transferring the gasworks from Edinburgh to Granton.

In private, Mr Kinloch Anderson was held in high regard by a wide circle of friends for his business ability and courteous and kindly disposition. He is survived by a widow and by a family of six sons and three daughters.

At yesterday's meeting of The Water Trust, Lord Provost Steel referred to the great loss which the community had sustained by Mr Anderson's death, and Bailie Brown, the Senior Magistrate, spoke in similar terms at the opening of the Flower Show in the Waverley Market. The Bailie said he had entered the Town Council in the same year as his deceased colleague and could say that they would all feel that they had lost a personal friend. The Edinburgh Society of High Constables had arranged to have a general meeting for drill last night but out of respect to the memory of Mr Anderson, who was a past Moderator of the Society, Mr Bruce Fenwick, the Vice-Moderator, dissolved the meeting after roll had been called and the drill was abandoned.

The Scotsman – Tuesday November 19, 1901
Funeral of the late Mr WJ Kinloch Anderson

The funeral took place yesterday, from his residence, The Elms, Craigmillar Park to the Grange Cemetery, of the late Mr WJ Kinloch Anderson JP, DL, who was one of the representatives in the Town Council of Newington Ward.

In deference to the wishes of the family, the Town Council did not officially attend the funeral, but most of the members were present and also a large and representative gathering of businessmen, to show respect to the memory of this estimable citizen.

Service was conducted in the drawing room by the Reverend A Neil of the Church of Scotland, Mayfield and in the dining room by the Reverend W Morison, Rosehall United Free Church.

The funeral procession consisted of over sixty carriages, and as this imposing cortege proceeded along Mayfield, Grange Loan and Kilgraston Road to the cemetery, it attracted much notice. Along the route, many of the houses had their blinds drawn. At the grave, prayer was offered by the Reverend Dr Robertson, North Berwick and the pallbearers were the six sons and a nephew of the deceased. At a meeting of Newington Ward Municipal Committee last night in the Livingstone Hall, Clark Street a resolution was passed on the motion of the Reverend John Baird, seconded by Treasurer Cranston, expressing the committee's sense of the loss which the ward has sustained by the death of Mr Kinloch Anderson and their sympathy with the deceased councillor's family.

Below: The Town Council of Edinburgh, 1896. Bailie Anderson is seated fifth from left, in the front row.

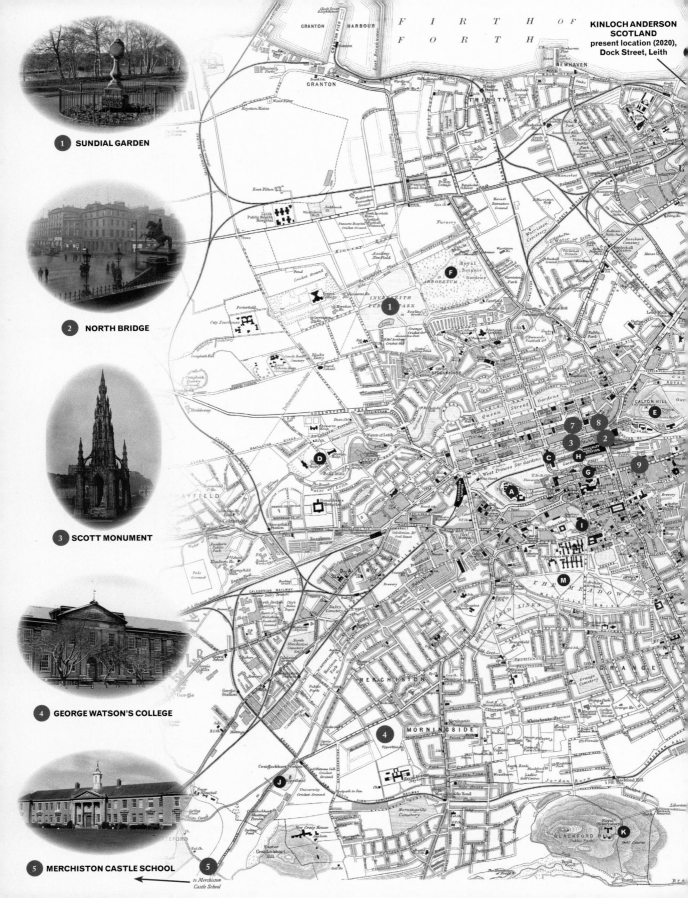

KINLOCH ANDERSON SCOTLAND present location (2020), Dock Street, Leith

1 SUNDIAL GARDEN

2 NORTH BRIDGE

3 SCOTT MONUMENT

4 GEORGE WATSON'S COLLEGE

5 MERCHISTON CASTLE SCHOOL

Kinloch Anderson's
EDINBURGH and LEITH

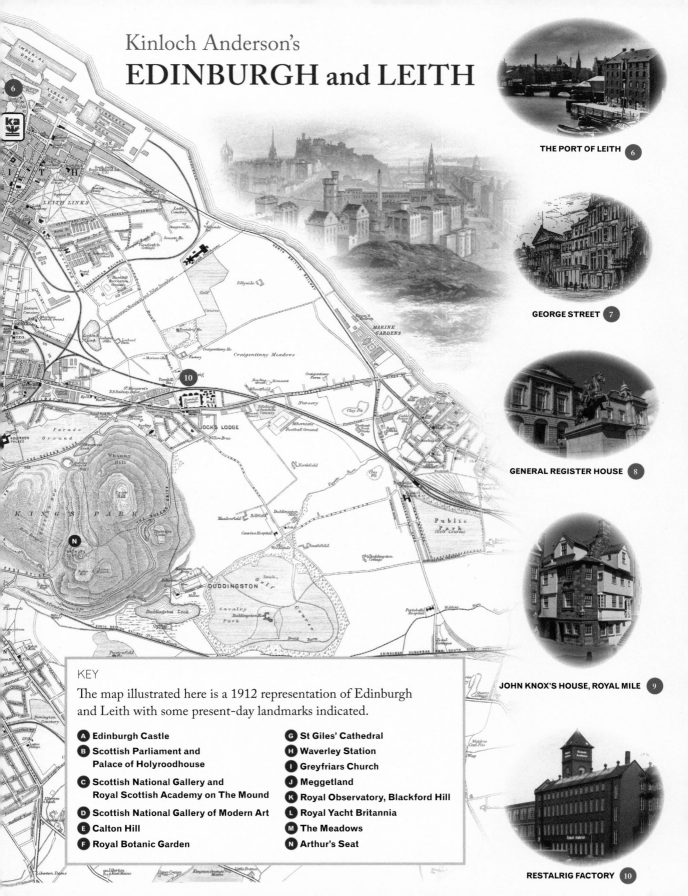

THE PORT OF LEITH 6

GEORGE STREET 7

GENERAL REGISTER HOUSE 8

JOHN KNOX'S HOUSE, ROYAL MILE 9

RESTALRIG FACTORY 10

KEY

The map illustrated here is a 1912 representation of Edinburgh and Leith with some present-day landmarks indicated.

A Edinburgh Castle

B Scottish Parliament and Palace of Holyroodhouse

C Scottish National Gallery and Royal Scottish Academy on The Mound

D Scottish National Gallery of Modern Art

E Calton Hill

F Royal Botanic Garden

G St Giles' Cathedral

H Waverley Station

I Greyfriars Church

J Meggetland

K Royal Observatory, Blackford Hill

L Royal Yacht Britannia

M The Meadows

N Arthur's Seat

Right: The partnership agreement of William Joseph Kinloch Anderson and Andrew Hislop Anderson, signed on July 31, 1878.

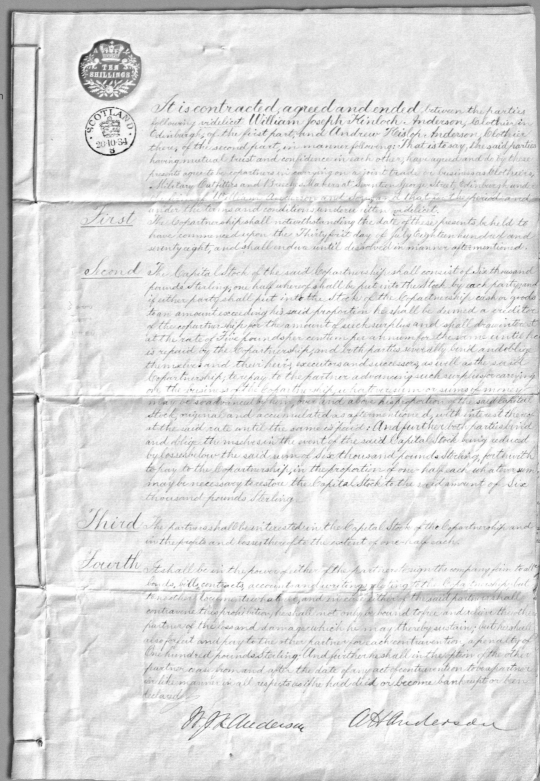

Wm Kinloch Anderson

W. Hislop Anderson

Chapter Three

WILLIAM KINLOCH ANDERSON AND WILLIAM HISLOP ANDERSON

THIRD GENERATION

KINLOCH ANDERSON
HEATHER TARTAN

T HE fathers of William Kinloch and William Hislop had both died suddenly within six months of each other, leaving their sons, in their early twenties, to take the responsibility for the company. This they did successfully despite very challenging times. Demands for their services grew, especially during the First World War, when vast quantities of uniforms for officers were produced by the company.

Records show that as many as 100 pieces of khaki cloth for making greatcoats were purchased at one time. It has to be remembered that every coat was cut by hand and made by skilled tailors by the traditional bespoke methods.

William Kinloch Anderson (1874–1949)

William Kinloch Anderson was the eldest son of William Joseph Kinloch Anderson and his wife Mary Wilson, who was the daughter of a very successful East Lothian farmer. He was baptised as plain William and it was only later that the Kinloch from his father's name was added. The Kinloch name was then passed as a Christian name to his son, fourth generation, who always used it and was known by it as his first name.

It was not until the fifth generation, Douglas Kinloch Anderson, that it was decided to change the name of the company from William Anderson & Sons Limited to Kinloch Anderson Limited, the name as it remains today. Kinloch Anderson Limited began in the 1950s when the company created

Page 59 and swatch above: Native to Scotland, heather has always been a Scottish symbol of good luck. The Kinloch Anderson Heather tartan presents shades of purple, green and grey, colours which pervade the landscape of the Scottish countryside.

Opposite: William Kinloch Anderson (left) and William Hislop Anderson (right).

a wholesale subsidiary for the export of Scottish clothing and accessories to North America and Bermuda.

As a child, William Kinloch Anderson spent his holidays on his grandfather's farm "Ballencrieff" near Aberlady. In a letter to Douglas Kinloch Anderson, William's daughter Elsa Rennie wrote, "in his mind the words Ballencrieff and Heaven were just the same".

William was taken into the business in 1890 by his "Victorian" father when he left George Watson's College at the age of sixteen. He was given very menial jobs, including sweeping out the shop. He also had to use a letter press to record correspondence. It was early in his business career when his father died, in 1901, and he inherited the family firm.

Below: How the George Street shop interior looked in the 1920s.

William married Ella MacGregor in 1900. She is remembered by her family as being forthright, energetic and lively. They had three children, William James Kinloch, Elsa Kinloch and Ronald Kinloch. Ella MacGregor's father ran the Star & Garter in Linlithgow and then became manager of the Rutland Hotel at Edinburgh's West End. She used to claim – as do many MacGregors – that she was descended from Rob Roy MacGregor!

Rather more likely, however, she also claimed a connection with Robert Burns. Her mother's mother was a Miss Burness (the manuscript in the Burns Museum in Alloway of the poet's first collection of poems describes them as by Robert Burness) and she was descended from Gilbert Burness (the brother of Burns) who became a factor to the Grant Estate in East Lothian. His handsome gravestone is in the kirkyard of East Bolton near Haddington.

William Kinloch was reserved and constrained his emotions. However, he was known to be kind and generous, always helping people with money but careful that the source was not revealed and his good deeds kept secret. When one of his tailors in George Street lost his life in the 1914–18 war, William Kinloch bought a small flat near Tollcross for his family and only asked for a small rent. He then employed the widow as additional domestic help for his family house "Torwood" in Colinton. "The company was his life and his great interest," wrote his daughter Elsa, "and in the evenings he used to talk about all the things that had happened."

William Kinloch Anderson was known always to be ready to help and give his advice. We are told that his staff admired him but sometimes with trepidation. He believed in discipline. This is confirmed by a small booklet "Rules and Regulations" which was issued to all members of staff.

Above: Elsa Rennie, the daughter of William Kinloch Anderson.

RULES AND INSTRUCTIONS.

1. Everyone must be in his or her place and business in full swing by 9 a.m.

2. All fixtures, table and warehouse dressing must be completed by 9-30 a.m.

3. Wrappers and Covers must not be put on until ten minutes before closing time.

4. Assistants will leave their Departments as seldom as possible, and never without seeing that someone is in charge.

5. Reason for absence from business must be notified at once.

6. All errors when discovered and all breakages, etc., must be reported immediately.

7. Assistants will not leave or enter either 14 or 16 George Street premises at any time by Rose Street entrance, except as arranged for in Rule 8.

8. Any Assistants requiring to go on Company's business to firms in Rose Street will leave by the ground level back door of No. 16, the key of which is kept hanging inside the glass door. The outside back door will be locked by them when they leave, and when they return, and the key returned to its place.

9. The back door of No. 14 George Street into Rose Street Lane will be closed every morning by the Caretaker at 9 a.m. and opened at 12-45 p.m., closed again at 2-30 p.m. and opened at 5-45 p.m. He will keep and be responsible for the key of this door.

1

Left and below: Rules and Instructions for Staff, issued in May of 1925.

Wᵐ ANDERSON & SONS Lᵗᵈ.
EDINBURGH AND GLASGOW.

RULES
and
INSTRUCTIONS
for
STAFF.

MAY 1925

> Dear Sirs
>
> We the undersigned would like to say a word of thanks for your kind recognition of our long service with the firm of Mess'' Anderson & Sons, first by the gift of money so acceptable & now by the presentation of the photograph, which we will have ever before us. We have all spent many years at George Street & hope that the relations between us, employee & employer will be just as amicable for the years remaining to us all. We would also express our loyalty & respect to Mr' Kinloch Anderson & Mr' Hislop Anderson & yourselves on the auspicious occasion you have just celebrated.
>
> We are
> Your faithful Servants.
> A. W. Stirling
> D.M. Alexander
> W D Maclennan
> N. Blyth
> J. Moyes
> J. Clark
> R. Ross
> John Perry
> John Mavor

The Veterans' Presentation, 1925

Over the years, Kinloch Anderson has enjoyed the loyalty and long service of its staff. On October 16, 1925, a presentation was made to several staff veterans, celebrating their many years of service with the company. The celebration comprised a dinner, a presentation, speeches and a dance.

That night, before he presented these "Long Service" awards, William Kinloch Anderson said, "I have now a very pleasing duty to perform. We have with us tonight the employees who have been with the firm each for thirty years and over. We have thought it a suitable opportunity to acknowledge this service and we have great pleasure in making a presentation to each of them to mark the occasion."

The staff honoured were James Clark (49 years service), John Perry (42 years), Alex W Stirling (37 years), Andrew Moffatt (35 years), Robert Ross (35 years), William D MacLennan (34 years), David M Alexander (34 years), John Moyes (32 years), John Mavor (30 years) and William Blyth (29 ½ years).

Mr Kinloch Anderson concluded with, "In presenting each, I tender our sincere regard for them and our thanks for the many years of faithful labour performed."

Above: This letter was written by long-serving staff of William Anderson & Sons to thank their employers for the 1925 "Presentation to Our Veterans", celebrating their many years of work for the company.

EVENTS DURING THE TIME OF THE THIRD GENERATION

1901 ▶ The death of Queen Victoria. ▶ Coronation of King Edward VII (1841–1910) and Queen Alexandra (1844–1925).

1902 ▶ The North British Hotel (now the Balmoral) was built in Edinburgh.

1903 ▶ A floral clock was unveiled in Princes Street Gardens. ▶ Emmeline (1858–1928) and Christabel Pankhurst (1880–1958) found the Women's Social and Political Union. ▶ Opening of Willow Tearooms in Sauchiehall Street, Glasgow.

1904 ▶ The Edinburgh Museum of Science and Art is renamed as the Royal Scottish Museum. ▶ Boroughmuir High School, Edinburgh, founded. ▶ Booklets of stamps first issued.

1907 ▶ Mahatma Ghandi (1869–1948) leads civil disobedience in South Africa.

1908 ▶ Mass demonstration of suffragettes. ▶ Boy Scout movement founded. ▶ Ernest Shackleton's (1874–1922) *Nimrod* expedition to South Pole.

Above: Staff of 1890. Front row: 2nd from left, James Clark; 4th from left, Alex Stirling. Both men can also be found in the picture below taken in 1925.

Above: A picture of Kinloch Anderson employees attending the Long Service award ceremony in 1925. A local newspaper commented: "A splendid record of service with one firm has been set up by nine employees of William Anderson & Sons Ltd, military outfitters, George Street, Edinburgh. From left to right they are: Back row – James Clark, Alex Stirling, William Blyth, John Moyes. Front – Robert Ross, John Perry, John Mavor, William D MacLennan and David M Alexander."

1909 ▶ Old Age Pensions Act comes into force.

1910 ▶ Girl Guides founded.

▶ Death of Edward VII. George V (1865–1936) becomes King.

1911 ▶ Coronation of King George V and Queen Mary in June of 1911. The King and Queen visit Edinburgh in July.

1914 ▶ The First World War (1914–18) begins.

▶ Irish Home Rule Act creates separate parliament in Ireland.

1915 ▶ In 1915, 227 men of the 7th (Leith) Battalion of the Royal Scots die on their way to fight in the Dardanelles. Their train crashes into a goods train at Gretna Junction.

▶ Harry Lauder (1870–1950, born Harold McLennon), famous for his songs "Roamin' in the Gloamin'" and "I Love a Lassie", is at the peak of his stardom.

Ready-To-Wear – A Bold Move

It was towards the end of the 1920s when William Anderson & Sons decided to set up a ready-to-wear department. This was a bold move which was derided and considered to be "going downmarket". In fact, the company was looking ahead and predicting future market trends. It incurred the disdain of the master tailoring companies in George Street. There were then seventeen such companies in George Street and by 1939 there were only three left!

William Anderson & Sons lost no time in establishing their ready-to-wear range which included men's lounge suits, jackets, raincoats and overcoats.

EVENTS DURING THE TIME OF
THE THIRD GENERATION

1916
▶ Conscription introduced in England.

▶ The Easter Rising in Ireland.

1917
▶ United States declares war on Germany.

▶ Women's Army Auxiliary founded.

▶ First German bombing raid on London.

▶ Order of the British Empire founded by King George V (1865–1936).

1918
▶ From 1918–19 the Spanish Flu pandemic kills millions, one of the deadliest pandemics in human history.

▶ Irish Parliament founded.

▶ Women over the age of thirty allowed to vote.

▶ Armistice signed by Germany.

1919
▶ German fleet of battleships scuttled at Scapa Flow, Orkney.

▶ Nancy Astor (1879–1964, right) is the first woman to take her seat in the House of Commons.

▶ Amritsar Massacre. 380 protesting Indians are killed, 1200 wounded, by British troops.

From a William Anderson & Sons Ltd promotional leaflet:

> *Every garment is guaranteed cut and tailored on the premises as opposed to the factory productions so generally offered elsewhere. Particular attention is drawn to the much larger range of lounge suits now available ready-to-wear. The quality of all goods offered in all departments is consistently high, whilst prices generally are more attractive than last year.*

In addition, William Anderson & Sons were also appointed as agents for the prestigious menswear companies of Burberry and Aquascutum.

On this spread: (From left to right) Company brochure *Outfitting for Men*, an Ulster wrap coat, a Raglan coat and an Aquascutum coat.

1920
▶ Conscription ends in England.

▶ Establishment of separate parliament for Northern Ireland.

▶ Bloody Sunday: IRA kill fourteen British soldiers.

▶ Admission of women to do degrees at Oxford University.

1921
▶ Anglo–Irish Treaty sets up Irish Free State. Division of former kingdom of Ulster into Northern Ireland.

▶ Opening of first Indian Parliament.

1922
▶ First double decker bus.
▶ First Corporate Tram.
▶ St Trinneans School opened in Palmerston Place (Margaret Kinloch Anderson's School).

1925
▶ Opening of new national Rugby Stadium at Murrayfield, the largest stadium in Scotland with a capacity of 67,000. (This was redeveloped 1992–94 with a £50 million overhaul and the old grandstand demolished for the new all-seater stadium of today.)

Tailored for Scotland

On this spread: (From left to right) A double-breasted chesterfield coat, a tweed jacket, a ready-to-wear lounge suit, a plus-four suit and an Aquascutum raincoat.

EVENTS DURING THE TIME OF
THE THIRD GENERATION

1926
▶ The General Strike attempts to force the government to prevent wage reduction for 1.2 million coal miners.

1927
▶ First non-stop transatlantic flight made by Charles Lindbergh (1902–74).

▶ Demonstration of colour television in Glasgow.

▶ First automatic telephone service in London.

1928
▶ Edinburgh's Empire Theatre reopened after a fire.

▶ Alexander Fleming (1881–1955) discovers Penicillin.

▶ Amelia Earhart is first woman to fly the Atlantic.

▶ Women over the age of twenty-one allowed to vote on same basis as men.

1929
▶ The Wall Street Crash: 16 million shares are sold and the US economy collapses. The repercussions are felt all around the world.

1930

▶ The consequence of US banks extending too many bad loans sparks the Great Depression of the 1930s.

▶ Mahatma Gandhi (1869–1968) begins his civil disobedience campaign against British rule in India.

1932
▶ Amelia Earhart (1897–1937) completes solo transatlantic flight.

1934
▶ The National Party of Scotland and the Scottish Party merge to form the Scottish National Party (SNP).

1938
▶ Commercial launch of the artificial fibre Nylon. Mainly developed by Wallace Carothers (1896–1937) with a team of researchers at US company DuPont.

The Company of Merchants of the City of Edinburgh

Master of the Merchant Company

William Kinloch Anderson was distinguished both in appearance and in ability and he became a Justice of the Peace. At one point, he had to choose between becoming the Lord Provost of the City of Edinburgh or the Master of the Merchant Company. He chose the Merchant Company of which he was Master from 1936–1938. During this time, on one occasion he was to attend a dinner at which the Duke of Kent was the guest of honour. William Kinloch Anderson's daughter, Elsa Rennie, wrote in a letter to her nephew Douglas recalling that her father came downstairs wearing immaculate evening clothes, and as he put on his overcoat he said, "This is the peak of my career."

The Scotsman, **Friday October 16, 1936**

MERCHANT COMPANY
NOMINATION OF NEW MASTER – MR W KINLOCH ANDERSON

"A man of the utmost profound integrity and a business man of capacity," was how Mr R H Munro described Mr William Kinloch Anderson, who was nominated as the next Master of the Edinburgh Merchant Company, at a meeting held yesterday in the Merchants' Hall, Hanover Street, Edinburgh. Mr Munro, the present Master of the Company, in proposing his successor, said that two years ago, when he proposed Mr Anderson as the new Treasurer, he did so knowing full well that he was one widely known as a man of profound integrity, a business man of capacity and one who in the administration of the Company's affairs would have vision, breadth of view and kindly common sense. "Two friendly and very busy years of close working with him have come and gone," said Mr Munro, "and I am more than ever convinced that Treasurer Anderson as Master, will fill the position not only with great acceptance to the members, but in a manner proper to the traditions and the importance of the Company" [Applause]. Lord Dean Of Guild Wilson seconded the proposal.

The Royal Company of Merchants of the City of Edinburgh

The Royal Company of Merchants of the City of Edinburgh (previously the Company of Merchants of the City of Edinburgh) has a rich history interwoven with the fabric of Edinburgh life for over 300 years. In its early days, the Company concerned itself with such matters as the city water supply and expressed regret that too many trading premises were being turned into "brandy shops" or "tippling places". However, eventually the status and influence of members was seen by public-spirited benefactors as an efficient and perpetual means of putting into effect their last wills and testaments and, as a result, charitable trusts were left to the Company to administer.

This, coupled with shrewd investment, resulted in the Company becoming one of the biggest landowners in Scotland. For example, one of the Master's responsibilities was that of the Chairman of the Trustees of the Harbours of Peterhead and Chairman of the Managers of the Feuars of Peterhead. It also saw the Company assuming responsibilities, relating mainly to the young, the poor and the elderly. In 1694 Mary Erskine, possibly the widow of a Company Member, gave over 10,000 merks* for the "maintenance of burgess female children", which established the Mary Erskine School. Further legacies resulted in the opening of George Watson's College in 1741, Daniel Stewart's College in 1855 and James Gillespie's High School (the latter was handed over to the management of the Edinburgh School Board in 1908).

As time passed, the focus of the Company moved completely to education and charitable works. Since the Company came into being, it has had three principal homes: the first in the Cowgate, the second in Hunter Square and the current Merchant's Hall in Hanover Street. However, there were a number of years when the Company met in various coffee houses in the city whilst without a permanent home. In 1879 the Glasgow Bank failed and its offices came on the market at 22 Hanover Street and were purchased by the Company. Over the years, whilst the original façade remains (it is a listed structure of special architectural and historical interest), it has been renovated extensively internally to suit the Company's changing needs.

However, in the Secretary and Chamberlain's room, there remains a link with Hunter Square Merchant's Hall. The decorative mantelpiece was brought from there, with its main feature a representation of the sailing ship so important in the Company coat of arms.

The Merchant Company has been fortunate to have a long-standing relationship with the Royal Family. Her Majesty The Queen is the Company Patron, His Royal Highness The Duke of Edinburgh was Master in 1965 and HRH The Princess Royal was Master in 2003. 2019 was the seventieth anniversary of HM The Queen becoming an Honorary Member. In the previous year, the Queen granted the Company the singular privilege of adding "royal" to its name. Today, the Royal Company of Merchants continues its work of educating the young through its flourishing schools and grant-awarding funds. It looks after the elderly through personal support, grants and the provision of modern social housing. It has an active membership of over 500 senior business figures in Edinburgh and is innovative in its financial support of young business people in the city. As well as its rich past, all this ensures that the Royal Company of Merchants has a significant role to play in Edinburgh life for many generations to come.

* The merk (abolished in 1707) was a Scottish silver coin, with value two thirds of a Scottish pound, or 13 shillings and 4 pence.
Below: The Merchants' Hall, the Royal Company of Merchants, Edinburgh.

William Kinloch Anderson died on February 5, 1949 and will be remembered for his exceptional contributions both to his company and to his city.

WJ Kinloch Anderson wrote of the death of his father William Kinloch Anderson in the company's 1949 annual report:

> *"I hope I may be pardoned for expressing my personal pride in the long and valued service which my late father gave, not only to this company, but to the tailoring trade in Scotland generally. He was associated with the company for sixty years, which time he completed on January 22nd of this year, just about a fortnight before his death. Along with the late Mr W Hislop Anderson, he was undoubtedly the architect of the company as we have known it in the years gone by, and the success and reputation achieved by the company was in no small measure due to his business capacity, acumen and shrewd judgement. Although in latter years his health was failing, he retained the keenest personal interest in the business right till the end."*

William Hislop Anderson (c.1875–1948)

William Hislop Anderson was the cousin of William Kinloch Anderson and his partner in the company. He took the responsibility for the tailoring and clothing production and he was known for his interest in the welfare of all the employees of the company.

William Hislop Anderson was also involved in the Edinburgh Merchant Company, admitted as a member in December 1917. In 1923 he was elected Trades Councillor to the Convenery of Edinburgh and re-elected in 1924. The Convenery of the Trades of Edinburgh consists of the Deacons of all the incorporated trades, and today acts as the ruling body of the Incorporated Trades.

At the celebration event held in 1925 for the William Anderson & Sons veterans (which has already been referred to), William Hislop reminisced about his own tailoring education in a thank-you letter (*see* opposite page) to Miss Elliot, one of the secretaries. The occasion was also an opportunity for "Mr William and Mr Hislop" and their wives to be presented with twenty-fifth wedding anniversary gifts, but Mr Hislop was too ill to attend. In his letter he writes of his own thirty years at the company and working with the men who were already long-serving and loyal employees. He conveys his own affectionate memories of working with them and also learning from them. "Outside the work rooms there is no one connected with the company who has known them as long as I have," he wrote.

The veterans' celebration showed the mutual respect and affection held between the managing partners and their employees whose years of service is evidence of their loyalty to the company.

Above: William Hislop, aged 22 and later in life.

October 16th, 1925

Dear Miss Elliot,

I am greatly disappointed not to be with you tonight but the Doctor says NO! I hope you will have a successful and enjoyable evening.

I, of course know of the presentation which is to be made to Mrs Anderson and myself on this our Silver Wedding Year. We know of the very handsome present the employees of the company have arranged to give us, and we thank you one an all for your good wishes and kindness. We appreciate most the spirit of friendliness and esteem which prompted it.

While regretting very much my inability to be present and thank you personally, I think I am even more disappointed at not being able to take part in the Presentation to our Veterans. Outside the work rooms there is no one connected with the company who has known them as long as I have. They were all young or very young men 30 years ago when I also was of the latter class. They all worked under my charge in those days and, looking back, all I can remember are the many pleasant and laughable things that happened and none of the differences which of course, were bound to occur. If I had been with you tonight I had intended telling you of some of these incidents. These were the days of old Cowan, old Calder, McKenzie, Culbert, Munro, Cochrane, Jack Robertson and many others.

One of the nicest things ever said to me was by Jack Robertson. It was a few years after my father's

Above: Receipts of gifts to "Mr William" and "Mr Hislop". In 1925 they were both presented with wedding anniversary presents by their staff.

death; he was standing beside me in the Cutting Room, had just received instruction regarding an elaborate military Mess Waistcoat he was making, when he said, "Man, ye ken ye are doing verra weel; we have made a guid job of ye and we are proud of ye."

It was that "we" as much as anything else; these Veterans in the firm's service whom we are honouring today are part of that body comprised by Robertson's "we".

Employer and employee, in this long period of working together, are paying each other the greatest compliments. I wish them all many years of health and happiness.

Again thanking you all on behalf of Mrs Anderson and myself,

I am,

Yours sincerely,

W Hislop Anderson.

Andrew Hislop Anderson (1885–1979)

Whilst his elder brother William Hislop had joined William Anderson & Sons, Andrew Hislop joined a shipping company and travelled the world. He was the first member of the family to leave Scotland never to return, and the first to marry other than "a Scottish lass". He settled in Berkeley Oregon in the USA, marrying an English girl, Charlotte Elizabeth Robinson (1892–1967) in 1913.

The consequence of US banks extending too many bad loans, and the Wall Street Crash of 1929, contributed to the Great Depression of the 1930s. The Depression hit Andrew hard, like many people, and put an end to many of his hopes and goals. However, Kathleen Elizabeth Glover writes with great admiration of her grandfather, "In spite of financial losses, he maintained his dignity and perseverance, the same innate qualities that his employers spoke of in his youth in Scotland. Each one of us can only hope that when faced with life's hardships we can show the same strength as Andrew exhibited."

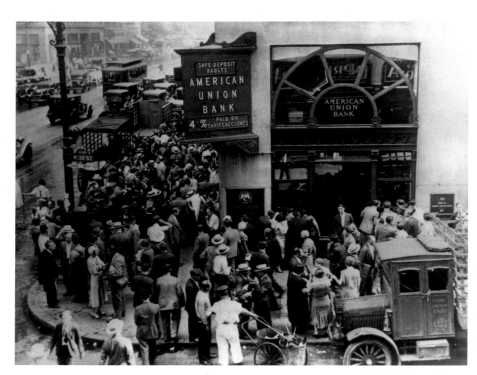

Right: A crowd at New York's American Union Bank during a bank run early in the Great Depression.

The bank opened in 1917 and went out of business on June 30, 1931.

Uniforms for the Services

WM. ANDERSON & SONS LTD
EDINBURGH   GLASGOW
SCOTLAND

Chapter Four

MILITARY AND CIVILIAN UNIFORMS

KINLOCH ANDERSON
ROWANBERRY TARTAN

"Uniform making is the work of specialists and requires experience, skill and accurate records."

Uniforms for the Services leaflet, 1928/1930

KINLOCH Anderson's military outfitting dates back to 1868. From that time, William Anderson & Sons made many of the official uniforms for the voluntary brigades. However, it was under the leadership of William Kinloch Anderson (1874–1949) that bespoke military tailoring developed still further as such an important part of the business. The company made the officers' uniforms for all the Scottish regiments.

The scope of the company's expertise with uniform was extensive. They made uniforms for the Regular Army, the Territorial Army, the Royal Navy, the Royal Navy Volunteer Reserves (RNVR), the Royal Air Force, the Civil and Diplomatic Corps (including Lord Lieutenants and Deputy Lieutenants, the Royal Company of Archers [KBGS], Consular and Civil uniforms and Court dress).

Other civilian outfitting included hunting and hacking kit for riders and, in addition, the stores stocked travelwear such as washing suits (suits that could be washed), tropical worsted suits, tropical dress clothes, underwear, sheets and pillows, and camping gear.

Page 75 and the swatch above: In Celtic mythology, the Rowanberry tree was referred to as the "tree of life". In Scotland, the berries of the Rowan Tree are red, whereas in Asia there are some species where they are a golden yellow. The Kinloch Anderson Rowanberry tartan is predominantly red with a yellow overcheck and links the Kinloch Anderson Company to its business partners in Asia.

Opposite: A William Anderson & Sons brochure, *Uniforms for the Services*, from 1928/1930.

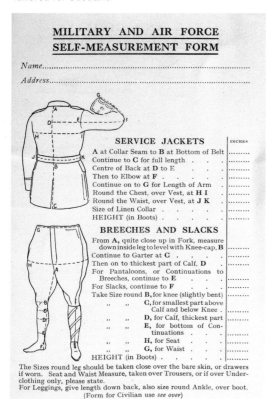

MILITARY AND AIR FORCE SELF-MEASUREMENT FORM

Name..

Address..

SERVICE JACKETS

	INCHES
A at Collar Seam to **B** at Bottom of Belt	....
Continue to **C** for full length	....
Centre of Back at **D** to **E**	....
Then to Elbow at **F**	....
Continue on to **G** for Length of Arm	....
Round the Chest, over Vest, at **H I**	....
Round the Waist, over Vest, at **J K**	....
Size of Linen Collar	....
HEIGHT (in Boots)	....

BREECHES AND SLACKS

	INCHES
From **A**, quite close up in Fork, measure down inside leg to level with Knee-cap, **B**	....
Continue to Garter at **C**	....
Then on to thickest part of Calf, **D**	....
For Pantaloons, or Continuations to Breeches, continue to **E**	....
For Slacks, continue to **F**	....
Take Size round **B**, for knee (slightly bent)	....
,, ,, **C**, for smallest part above Calf and below Knee	....
,, ,, **D**, for Calf, thickest part	....
,, ,, **E**, for bottom of Continuations	....
,, ,, **H**, for Seat	....
,, ,, **G**, for Waist	....
HEIGHT (in Boots)	....

The Sizes round leg should be taken close over the bare skin, or drawers if worn. Seat and Waist Measure, taken over Trousers, or if over Underclothing only, please state.
For Leggings, give length down back, also size round Ankle, over boot.
(Form for Civilian use *see over*)

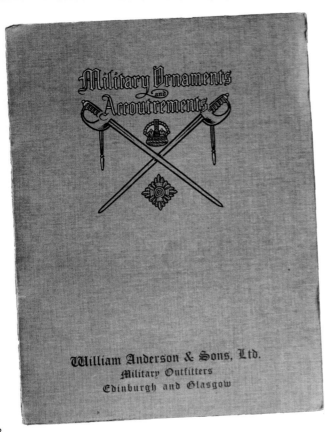

Military Ornaments and Accoutrements

William Anderson & Sons, Ltd.
Military Outfitters
Edinburgh and Glasgow

From *Uniforms for the Services* leaflet, 1928/1930

A Record of Service

For all these years' service of a high order has been given to Military Officers – First to the old Volunteer and Yeomanry Regiments, then at the time of the Boer War to the Regulars, Militia, Yeomanry and Volunteers. A reputation as military outfitters of the highest class was confirmed and enhanced during the Great War, when uniform was made for innumerable Officers of Scottish and other Regiments, as well as for the Royal Navy and the Royal Airforce. Since the War, progress has been maintained and every outfitting need of Officers can be satisfied.

Today Anderson's are Regimental outfitters to all the Scottish Regiments and are widely recognised as the premier uniform makers in Scotland. The number of Regular Officers being supplied with uniform and Equipment has never been larger.

The Royal Navy and RNVR (Royal Navy Volunteer Reserves)

We have many customers in the Navy, especially among those who appreciate excellent workmanship. Our RNVR clientele in Scotland is extensive. First-class materials, workmanship and lacing, contribute to your success.

From *Outfitting for Men* leaflet, 1937

The Territorial Army

We are without question the leading firm in Scotland for Territorial Uniform, making for a large proportion of Serving Officers and for the majority of officers on first appointment. The Uniform we make is tailor-made and vastly superior to the factory-made qualities offered elsewhere. As the leading Scottish firm we make it our business to know exactly what is correct.

Left: A William Anderson & Sons brochure detailing Military Ornaments and Accoutrements.

From *Outfitting for Men* leaflet, Spring 1936

The Regular Army

Uniform Making is a branch of tailoring which demands specialist knowledge and experience, and especially is this so in the case of Scottish Uniform. We are the only firm in Scotland officially recognised by the officers of the Scottish Highland and Lowland regiments.

We make a large proportion of the first outfits for Officers joining Scottish Regiments from Sandhurst, and number among our regular customers most of the Senior Officers of all regiments. In addition, we are recognised by the RASC as Outfitters for Officers joining this Corps and make also for Officers of the RAMC, RC of S, Indian Army, or any other unit.

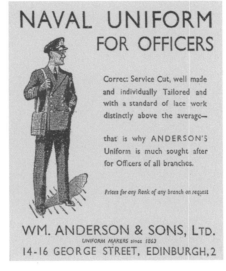

The Royal Air Force

We make uniform for a great number of officers in Scotland, both RAF Officers stationed here and Officers of the different Auxiliary Squadrons. Everything we supply is guaranteed correct in every detail and of first-class fit and finish.

We have made new pattern Mess Kit for a great many Officers and can supply this or convert the old pattern at moderate prices.

THE ILLUSTRATED LONDON NEWS,

On July 17, 1911, King George V and Queen Mary (whose coronation was on June 22, 1911) made their first state visit to Scotland. They stayed at their official Scottish residence, the Palace of Holyroodhouse, during their stay in Edinburgh. An extract from a supplement to *The Illustrated London News* talks of William Anderson & Sons' contribution to the day, specifically mentioning William Kinloch Anderson and William Hislop Anderson by name. The plethora of military uniforms on show was quite a spectacle, and many of those would have been made by William Anderson & Sons.

From a Supplement to *The Illustrated London News*, July 22, 1911:

MESSRS. WILLIAM ANDERSON AND SONS

The military spirit which was so strongly emphasised during the Coronation in London was not less conspicuous during the ceremonials attendant upon His Majesty's visit to Edinburgh. Uniforms flourished everywhere. Naturally all the famous regiments were represented but in accordance with the fitness of things, Scottish uniforms predominated. Here were men of the famous Black Watch, there the scarcely less celebrated Seaforth and Gordon Highlanders. Side-by-side with the

Below: Dense crowds populate Princes Street and Lothian Road awaiting the procession of King George V and Queen Mary.

tartan of the *Argyll and Sutherland and Cameron Highlanders was the picturesque uniform of the "Royal Company of Archers, the King's Bodyguard for Scotland" to give "this interesting survival of other days" its full title. Many of the uniforms of these and of other notable regiments were made by Messrs. William Anderson and Sons who have a great vogue as military tailors. Their fame is not confined to Scotland, but extends to the farthest quarters of the globe.*

Above: The Seaforth Highlanders awaiting the King's procession to the Palace of Holyroodhouse.

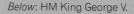

Below: HM King George V.

WM. ANDERSON & SONS, LTD., HOPE STREET, GLASGOW, C. 2

EQUIPMENT FOR OTHER RANKS

We deal extensively with Regimental Master Tailors, with Regiments themselves, and with Sergeants' Messes for the supply in quantity of equipment for other ranks.

We are able to offer very keen prices for quantities of

FEATHER BONNETS
For Bands or Rank and File Full Dress.

FEATHER HACKLES
(for use abroad in Officers' and Rank and File Topees). We supply many thousands each year to different Regiments.

GLENGARRIES
HOSE AND HOSE TOPS
SPORRANS
STAFF AND OFFICERS' TARTAN

Please ask for Particulars and Quotations.

21

This page and opposite: Details from the *Uniforms for the Services* booklet.

Continued from a Supplement to *The Illustrated London News*, July 22, 1911

The spirit of militarism pervading the whole of Messrs. Anderson's establishment has been the growth of more than forty years, and the present partners, Messrs. William Kinloch Anderson and William Hislop Anderson, may well be proud of their position. Inheriting a fine reputation, they have increased it by the finest business qualities, coupled with courtesy and fair dealing, and by giving their personal attention to every detail.

The founder of the firm was the late Mr William Anderson who began the business in 1868, at 15, George Street. He was joined soon afterwards by his two sons, Mr William J Kinloch Anderson (in his time a Bailie of the City of Edinburgh) and Mr Andrew Hislop Anderson, who, like their father are now dead. It was about twenty years ago that the existing partners entered the firm, when it removed to its present, large, well-lighted and handsomely appointed quarters at 14, George Street.

Military outfitting is, of course, the mainstay of the business, but it has also a fine reputation for civil tailoring, with breeches and hunting garments as specialties.

Uniforms had a particular attraction for the firm from the outset. In fact, some of the first orders were for this class of goods, many of them being for Volunteer regiments. At that time, privates as well as officers provided their uniforms at their own expense.

The military department of the firm probably received its greatest impetus, in recent years, during the latter part of 1899 and the years 1900 and 1901 – the period of the South African War, when very large numbers of outfits were made for all arms of the services.

The firm naturally supplies all the Highland and other Scottish regiments, the production of the Feather Bonnet worn by the latter being one of its special features. It likewise stocks the tartan for all regiments which wear them, as well as the elaborate ornaments like dirks, sgian dubhs, brooches etc, which go to finish off the civil as well as the military dress.

Besides the uniforms for regiments such as the English Infantry of the Line, the Royal Engineers and the Royal Artillery, the firm has especially laid itself out to serve the Territorial Battalions and other regiments, as the Royal Army Medical Corps, the Army Service Corps, etc, in addition to providing the uniforms of Indian and Colonial regiments. Messrs. Anderson also supply Court dress, Diplomatic uniforms and, in short, every uniform worn in the United Kingdom and the Colonies.

Some five years ago, a branch was opened at 196, St Vincent Street, Glasgow and it is a great success. Now the firm is breaking fresh ground in Canada, where there is great demand from the many Militia regiments which have adopted the uniform of Scottish regiments wearing the kilt. Its large clientele includes men in Africa, India, the Far East, Australia, New Zealand, Canada and the United States. In fact, the name of William Anderson and Sons is known in military circles wherever the English language is spoken.

Old Military Prints in our possession
at George Street, Edinburgh

Below: Items in the Kinloch Anderson Heritage Room.
(Left to right) Regimental sporrans; sgian dubhs, sporrans and shoes supplied to overseas regiments; a Royal Company of Archers uniform (Civilian).

Below: An illustration from *Records of the Scottish Volunteer Force*, by Sir James Moncrieff Grierson.

From *Outfitting for Men* leaflet, 1930

Civilian, Naval, Military, Airforce

For over fifty years our knowledge of this highly important branch of the business has been accumulating while we make uniforms for all branches of the Service, and it is a pleasure to advise Officers.

While we make uniforms for all branches of the Service – Navy, Army and Airforce – we naturally specialise in the production of kit for Scottish and Highland Regiments.

It is a pleasure to advise Officers as to the kit required and it is our business to submit estimates and details on request. All prices, bearing in mind that quality is of the highest, will be found strictly moderate.

Estimates for Lords Lieutenant, Deputy Lieutenants, all Civil, Court and Diplomatic Uniforms, also for Royal Company of Archers (KBGF) will be supplied on request without obligation to order.

| ENSIGN
4th SUTHD. R.V.
1860 | PRIVATE
1st SUTHD. R.V.
1860 | PRIVATE
3rd SUTHD. R.V.
1863–67 | PRIVATE
2nd CAITHNESS R.V.
1864–70 | CAPTAIN
1880–99 | PIPER
1883–1908 | PRIVATE
1899–1908 |

1ST SUTHERLAND V.R.C.

William Anderson & Sons, Ltd.
Military Outfitters
Edinburgh and Glasgow

Left and right: Promotional booklets.

Below: Buglers from the Queen's Rifle
Volunteer Brigade, 1885.

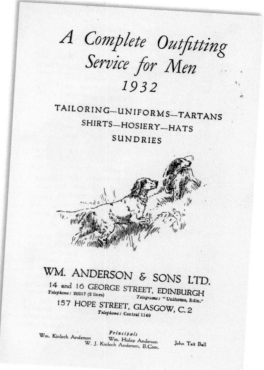

Officers' Uniforms
for Scottish Regiments

In the early part of the 20th century, Kinloch Anderson supplied officers' uniforms for all the famous Scottish regiments. Each regiment had its own tartan identity:

The Hunting Stewart tartan worn by the Royal Scots.

The Government tartan worn by the Royal Scots Fusiliers.

The Leslie tartan worn by the King's Own Scottish Borderers.

The Douglas tartan worn by the Cameronians.

The Government tartan (Black Watch sett) worn by the Black Watch (Royal Highlanders).

The MacKenzie tartan (Highland Light Infantry sett) worn by the Highland Light Infantry.

The MacKenzie tartan (Seaforth sett) worn by the Seaforth Highlanders.

The Gordon tartan worn by the Gordon Highlanders.

The Cameron of Erracht tartan worn by the Queen's Own Cameron Highlanders.

The Government tartan (Sutherland sett) worn by the Argyll and Sutherland Highlanders.

On March 28, 2006 the last four remaining regiments were amalgamated into the Royal Regiment of Scotland and the Government 1A (Black Watch) tartan was adopted as its regimental tartan.

The Royal Scots

The Royal Scots Fusiliers

The Highland Light Infantry

The Seaforth Highlanders

The King's Own Scottish Borderers

The Cameronians

The Black Watch (Royal Highlanders)

The Gordon Highlanders

The Queen's Own Cameron Highlanders

The Argyll and Sutherland Highlanders

Clockwise, from top left: Ties and squares in regimental colours; a complete set of regimental ornaments; advertising graphic for military overcoat; a clipping from the *Uniforms for the Services* leaflet.

WM. ANDERSON & SONS, LTD., GEORGE STREET, EDINBURGH 2

REGIMENTAL COLOURS

Ties and Squares for all Highland and Lowland Scottish Regiments, R.A., R.E., R.A.F., etc. Any colours can be supplied.
Ties, *from* 5/6, also in "Non-Crease" Silk, *from* 6/6; Squares, *from* 21/-
26   *Designs and Estimates for new colours on request.*

WM. ANDERSON & SONS, LTD., GEORGE STREET, EDINBURGH 2

REGIMENTAL ORNAMENTS

WM. ANDERSON & SONS Lᵗᵈ
EDINBURGH & GLASGOW

Complete Sets of Ornaments—Sporrans, Dirk, Skean Dhu, Shoulder Brooch, Full Dress Belts, and Shoe Buckles for every Scottish Regiment. First-grade workmanship and absolute accuracy are guaranteed.
Estimates and Designs for PIPE BANNERS on request.
10

SCOTTISH

As the Premier Uniform Makers in Scotland, Uniform for Officers of the

HIGHLAND AND LOWLAND REGIMENTS

has naturally been a matter for our special attention.

Our long experience has enabled us to gather together the fullest details of Regulations. Regulations for different Units vary considerably, and often there are differences between two Battalions of the same Regiment. We are in constant touch with the various Regiments, and the fact that we are frequently making Uniform for many of the Senior Officers, enables us to keep our information up to date.

Our Kit, besides being well tailored and correct in Regulation, is really smartly cut.

The following Regiments recognise us as their Regimental Tailors in Scotland :—
Royal Scots.   K.O.S.B.   Cameronians.   Black Watch. H.L.I.   Seaforth Highlanders.   Cameron Highlanders. Argyll and Sutherland Highlanders.

Young Officers who have just been granted a Commission may purchase their Kit from us with every confidence.

We guarantee absolute accuracy.

Our Representative visits the various Regiments at frequent intervals.

WILLIAM **ANDERSON** & SONS LTD.

4

The Cording Service Waterproof Coat

A TRUSTWORTHY WATERPROOF FOR MOUNTED AND GENERAL MILITARY WEAR IS A NECESSITY.

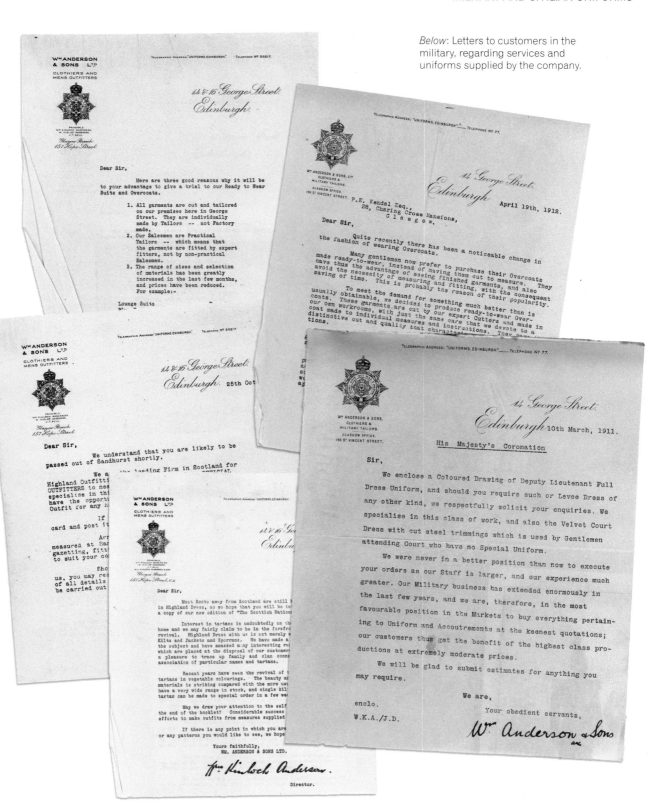

Below: Letters to customers in the military, regarding services and uniforms supplied by the company.

Above: Lieutenant Frederick Kinloch Anderson.

Above: Captain Walter Kinloch Anderson.

Family Losses During the First World War

Between 1914 and 1918, the Kinloch Anderson family lost four members who were serving in Scottish regiments.

Lieutenant Frederick Kinloch Anderson, Black Watch (Royal Highlanders)

Lieutenant Frederick Kinloch Anderson was one of nine children to Bailie William Joseph Kinloch Anderson and his wife Mary. He was born in 1880 and attended George Watson's College from 1886 to 1896. He was engaged in the engineer's department of the North British Railway when war broke out. Enlisting in the 9th Royal Scots, he received a commission in the 4th Royal Highlanders on 1915 and fell in Flanders in September of the same year.

Captain Walter Kinloch Anderson, Black Watch (Royal Highlanders)

Captain Walter Kinloch Anderson, a younger brother of Frederick Kinloch Anderson, was born in 1885 and attended George Watson's College from 1891 to 1902. He attended Edinburgh University, then qualified as a Chartered Accountant and before the outbreak of war was Joint Secretary of the Edinburgh Watsonian Club. He enlisted in 1915 and was commissioned to the 5th Royal Highlanders in March 1915. He was Bombing Officer for his Brigade from 1916 to 1918 and rose to be Captain. Crossing to France in April 1918, he was attached to the 6th Royal Highlanders, then a unit in the famous 51st Division. In the desperate fighting in the Bois de Courtrai he was killed on July 22, 1918.

Lance Corporal Walter Zerub Baillie Anderson, Royal Scots

Lance Corporal Walter Zerub Baillie Anderson was one of ten children to Andrew Hislop Anderson and his wife Joanna. He was born in 1888 and attended George Watson's College from 1894 to 1904. He was employed by William Anderson & Sons at the time of the outbreak of the war. Enlisting in the 15th Royal Scots, he was promoted to Lance Corporal and was wounded in France on April 1, 1916 and died two days later.

Lieutenant Eric MacLeod Milroy, Black Watch (Royal Highlanders)

Lieutenant Eric Milroy was one of four children to Alexander MacLeod Milroy and his wife Margaret Walteria, grandparents of the mother of Sir Eric, Douglas and Jane Kinloch Anderson; indeed, Eric was named after him. Eric Milroy was born in 1887 and attended George Watson's College from 1895–1906. At school he was an outstanding student, rugby player and debater, and he was a sergeant in the School Cadet Corps. He won an open bursary for mathematics to Edinburgh University and graduated with an honours degree. Shortly after the outbreak of the war, in September 1914 he joined the 9th Royal Scots from the Watsonian Training Corps. In January 1915 he was gazetted Second Lieutenant in the 11th Royal Highlanders and was engaged in severe fighting in the West Flanders Province at Ypres in France. In July 1916 he became a Lieutenant in the 8th Royal Highlander as Lewis Gun Officer. He lost his life in the Battle of the Somme in July 1916.

Above: Lieutenant Eric Milroy.

1914 – When the War Broke Out

In the first few memorable days of August, just after the war broke out, the outlook for retail traders in Edinburgh was of a gloomy character.

They lost a considerable portion of the tourist traffic; people at home, with the prospect of facing a prolonged and ruinous conflict, began to economise. Indeed, there were few in the city at that time who entertained the hope that hostilities would be over by Christmas.

With Christmas 1914 approaching, gift-giving was affected but it was made up to some extent by the purchases of comforts and other things to be sent to soldiers at the front or on duty at home. Had it not been for this, the old custom of giving Christmas presents would have been very seriously affected, resulting in a considerable loss for shopkeepers.

People had been much later in making their purchases. Some people had been feeling the pinch more than others. A notable example of this was the dressmaking trade, which was usually kept busy right up to Christmas.

There were not, of course, the same business conditions associated with Christmas as would have been the case in normal times, but considering the numerous calls made on people's pockets for a great variety of charities connected with the war, it was really wonderful how the business community did not suffer more at this time.

Haswell Miller Prints

In the 1950s the company was supplying officers' uniforms to the Scottish regiments in Canada and other Commonwealth countries. These are from a collection of five Haswell Miller Prints which were commissioned by the company in 1952. They were produced to check that every detail of the uniform was correct.

This spread: Argyll & Sutherland Highlanders, by Haswell Miller.

In the 1950s the company was supplying officers' uniforms to the Scottish regiments in Canada and other Commonwealth countries.

Archibald E Haswell Miller (1887–1979) was a Scottish Impressionist painter, modern artist, illustrator and curator. Born in Glasgow, he studied at the Glasgow School of Art, under Maurice Greiffenhagen and Jean Delville. He taught at this school of art from 1910 until 1930 when he became Deputy Director of the National Galleries of Scotland.

2ᵈ Bⁿ

1ˢᵀ Bⁿ.

2ⁿᴰ Bⁿ.

1ˢᵗ Bⁿ.

P. gulation wing

Regimental setteil.

PIPE MAJOR

Playing indoors

2ᵈ Battalion (93ᵈ)

(The bonnet is not worn but there is no reason why it should not be)

Review Order

(The sash is not usually worn thus in the A.93ᵈ. but over the right shoulder.)

Feather bonnet is not worn but there is no reason why it should not be.

Eagle feather in glengarry

Upper ribbon tartan Lower " green Pipe bags green.

Silver diamond buttons

Pipers have grey hair sporran.

Silver edge to leather tops and studs (3)

Sword seldom worn but should be.

PIPERS

Review Order

Playing indoors (Old uniform before the unfortunate introduction of the R. Stuart tartan for pipers)

A.E. Jarvisse Miller
Jan 1952

QUEEN'S OWN CAMERON HIGHLANDERS
79TH

The hackle should presumably now be blue.

Wings may have fringes or not.
Drummers and band should have black silk belts likes pipers

Sporran. Black hair. Top all leather.

Correct type of drum for a Royal Regiment

DRUMMERS OR BUGLERS

Review Order

Note that Drummers and Buglers head-dress must always be same as o.r. and not like band or pipers (if these differ). Also that fly plaid is correct – never belted plaid as worn by sergeants or officers

This spread: The Queen's Own Cameron Highlanders, by Haswell Miller.

As a painter, Miller specialised in portraits, landscapes and architecture. His work was exhibited at the Royal Scottish Academy and the Royal Academy. He was elected a member of the Royal Scottish Society of Painters in Watercolour in 1924.

As a young artist, he travelled across Europe to study painting. Having great interest in the military, he set out to record the colour and detail of many of the European armies.

Haswell Miller drew and painted hundreds of uniformed figures from these armies and became a recognised authority on the subject.

Above: An advertisement for women's service uniforms by William Anderson & Sons.

Women at War

At the time of the First World War, William Anderson & Sons were exclusively supplying uniforms for men. However, this advertisement (left) in *The Scotsman* (1940) clearly shows that this was no longer the case for the Second World War. Characteristically, the leadership of the family at this time adapted tailoring expertise to the changing requirements, and to responding to these new demands.

First World War

Women's first contributions to the First World War were limited to just a few voluntary organisations and official schemes, though thousands queued at labour exchanges to volunteer to help with the war effort.

By 1916, as army volunteer numbers dwindled, it was clear that the army needed conscription and the country needed women to fill the roles previously held by men, now fighting in the war. It suddenly became acceptable for women to be filling roles previously carried out by men. Women drove buses, worked in factories, made ammunitions and worked on the land. They filled military roles too.

They volunteered as nurses, going through several stages of medical training for nursing groups, such as the VADs (Voluntary Aid Detachments). 90,000 Red Cross volunteers worked at home and abroad. The primary role of the British Red Cross was to assist the naval and military medical services, treating sick and wounded sailors and soldiers.

As well as these auxiliary military duties, women were needed to work on the farms. The Women's National Land Services Corps (later the Women's Land Army) recruited women for jobs in farming and forestry.

The Women's Army Auxiliary Corps (the WAAC) was formed in December 1916. Women worked at home and on the fighting fronts as telephonists, telegraphers, typists, signallers, cooks, clerks, store-women, mechanics and drivers. The success of the corps led to the founding of the Women's Royal Naval Service (WRNS) and the Women's Royal Air Force (WRAF). By 1918 over 57,000 women had served in the WAAC (later renamed the QMAAC, Queen Mary's Army Auxiliary Corps), 5450 in the WRNS and 9000 in the WRAF.

Second World War

Once again war changed the world of work for women. Huge numbers of women were involved in the war effort and many volunteered to join the armed forces. Women were called up for war work from March 1941.

Initially, only single women aged 20–30 were called up, but by mid-1943, nearly 90 per cent of single women and 80 per cent of married women were involved working in factories, on the land or in the armed forces and providing essential air defence.

Over 640,000 British women served in the armed forces – in the Auxiliary Territorial Service (ATS), the Women's Auxiliary Air Force (WAAF) and the Women's Royal Naval Service (WRNS).

In the ATS they had roles such as cooks, store-women and orderlies, and later in the war, as radar operators and anti-aircraft gun crew members. The most notable member of the ATS during the Second World War was the then Princess Elizabeth. She trained as a driver and mechanic and reached the rank of Junior Commander.

At the onset of the war, the women's arm of the Royal Navy, the WRNS was reformed, known as "Wrens". They carried out a major part in the planning and organisation of naval operations, and they were involved in operating radar equipment and code-breaking at Bletchley Park.

In June 1939, the Women's Auxiliary Air Force was founded. WAAFs took on a variety of roles, including compiling weather reports, maintaining aircraft, serving on airfields and working in intelligence.

Many women flew unarmed aircraft, drove fire engines, ambulances and military vehicles. Others took up occupations as plumbers, nurses, train and tram conductors, or transported coal on barges.

From 1942, members of the Women's Timber Corps, known as "Lumber Jills", worked in forestry. Women worked in factories making aircraft parts and bombs, they worked in shipyards or as mechanics and engineers. More than 80,000 women formed the Women's Land Army, nicknamed the "Land Girls"; their work on farms was essential to prevent Britain from being "starved out".

The Women's Voluntary Service (WVS) were all non-uniformed volunteers.

Left: Auxillary Territorial Service, poster, 1939–1945.

Right: Examples of women in uniform during the Second World War.

Right: Air Raid Precautions poster from 1939.

Right: Air Raid Precautions poster from 1939.

In September 1939, the WVS managed the evacuation of schoolchildren all over the country. They were extremely active during the Blitz on London, attending to the basic needs of people whose homes were destroyed. They set up mobile canteen services during air raids and for troops moving through ports and railway stations, and undertook bandage-making, knitting and sewing essential clothing supplied to the front lines.

Around sixty women worked in the European resistance behind enemy lines as part of the Special Operations Executive. Often deployed by parachute or fishing boats, they were tasked to help form a "secret army" of resistance fighters to prepare the way for the Allied invasion.

All these women made a vital contribution to the war effort and triggered change in society's attitudes.

Right: John W Mills' "Monument to the Women of World War II", in Whitehall London.

The monument depicts the uniforms that women wore during the Second World War, symbolising the many roles they took on during wartime. They include a Women's Land Army uniform, a Women's Royal Naval Service uniform, a nursing cape, a police overall and a welding mask. Women had to give up these roles when the men returned from war.

Chapter Five

WILLIAM JAMES KINLOCH ANDERSON

FOURTH GENERATION

KINLOCH ANDERSON
BLUE LOCH TARTAN

WILLIAM James Kinloch Anderson (1907–1997) always used Kinloch as his first name. He was educated at Merchiston Castle School and then achieved a B.Com degree at Edinburgh University. In 1928 the curriculum for his course covered accounting and business method, organisation of industry and commerce, mercantile law, economic geography, economic history, French, industrial law and banking.

He was professional, peaceable, kindly and gentlemanly. He was also a good golfer and an active member of Mortonhall and Luffness Golf Clubs. Although he never became the Master of the Edinburgh Merchant Company, he greatly supported its invaluable involvement with the Edinburgh Merchant Company schools and was Vice Convener of George Watson's College. Like his predecessors, he always found time to make contributions to social welfare and fulfilled duties as an elder at St George's West Church on Sundays. He was a stalwart of the Boy Scout movement, first as a Scoutmaster, later as an administrator and in 1974 was awarded a Silver Acorn for his Services to Scouting.

Kinloch's wife, Margaret, was forthright, independently minded and educated at St Trinneans School. In her time, girls mostly did not go to university so she trained as a teacher and taught at the Royal Hospital for Sick Children in Edinburgh, locally known as the Sick Kids hospital. She was a Lieutenant in the Girl Guide movement and was for many years involved with running the Girl Guides in Colinton, Edinburgh, including their annual camps. She was intelligent, came from a professional family and would undoubtedly have had her own career in modern times.

Page 99 and above: Loch is the Gaelic word for lake and there are over 30,000 freshwater lochs in Scotland. The Kinloch Anderson Blue Loch tartan represents Scotland's lochs, rivers and coastlines. It also reflects the image of the Scottish flag which is blue with a white saltire cross.

Opposite: William James Kinloch Anderson.

The Wall Street Crash, 1929

From *Scotland: History of a Nation* **by David Ross**

The depression following the Wall Street crash of 1929 had a real impact on Scotland. Unemployment was as high as 30 per cent of the working population. In single-industry towns, this could mean something closer to 80 per cent.

This (with the exception of the scything down of so many of the young male population in 1914–1918) was the worst decade of the twentieth century for Scotland, beginning in financial instability and turning rapidly into industrial depression.

There was no evidence of competent management from a "national" government whose prime minister, in the early part of the decade, was a Scot himself, Ramsay Macdonald. Those who looked abroad to Europe saw only trouble. Even emigration, the answer so often before, had little to offer since the onetime lands of opportunity were themselves in slump. The crisis in the capital markets did not result in a Marxian revolt of the workers. Scotland was essentially a country of the working class, though the land-workers were less likely than industrial workers to see themselves in proletarian terms. Despite the apparent inability of government or the managerial class to improve matters, there were no great outbreaks of violent discontent. One or two Communist MPs were elected. The Labour Party had no cures to offer, drastic or otherwise. But even in 1932, when 27.7 per cent of the working population were unemployed, 72.3 per cent remained in work and had something to hold onto. For the rest, apart from their dole, if they qualified for it, and charitable handouts, there was a strong national tradition of grim endurance, with a special word to express it – they had to "thole" it and hope for better things to come.

Above: Crowd outside the New York City Stock Exchange, 1929.

EVENTS IN THE TIME OF THE FOURTH GENERATION

1937
▶ Death of Ramsay MacDonald (1866–1937), the first Labour Party politician to become Prime Minister of the UK.

1938
▶ Empire Exhibition Glasgow.

1939
▶ Germany Invades Poland. Second World War begins. Luftwaffe attacks shipping near the Forth Bridge – the first raid on Britain.

1940
▶ Introduction of food rationing.

▶ Winston Churchill (1874–1965) becomes Prime Minister of the UK.

▶ Evacuation of British Army from Dunkirk.

▶ Heavy German bombing of London; the Blitz.

1941
▶ Clothes rationing begins in the UK.

▶ Heavy bombing of London continues. The Chamber of the House of Commons is destroyed.

▶ In March, over two nights, German bombing devastates the town of Clydebank. 1200 are killed – Scotland's largest loss of civilian life. 35,000 are homeless.

▶ Japanese bombers attack Peal Harbour. Britain and USA declare war on Japan.

Kinloch and Margaret had three children, Eric, Douglas and Jane. The eldest son, Eric, was academically minded and, with a first-class honours degree in English from St Andrews University followed by a B.Litt at Oxford, chose a career in teaching. Jane took up nursing before she married an Episcopal Minister and had her own family. It was Douglas who joined the company as a young man of twenty-two years. Kinloch had never been given the control of the company until his own father died in 1949, so he gave Douglas plenty of opportunity to develop ideas for his own and the company's potential. It was a strong father–son partnership.

When the Wall Street Crash took place in 1929, WJ Kinloch Anderson was twenty-three years old. It would have been at this time that he followed his father into the company, by now a well-established Scottish clothing and military tailoring family business.

The next ten years were economically Scotland's worst in the twentieth century, as David Ross writes in *Scotland History of a Nation*, "beginning in financial instability and turning rapidly into industrial depression".

WJ Kinloch Anderson understood the recruitment problems facing the future of the tailoring trade in his time. Tailors were not high wage earners then, and this still applies in the 21st century. Whilst wages have progressed well for many other skills, the clothing industry has always sought the cheapest source of labour in whichever country of the world that can be found. Wages can only rise if the marketplace accepts the resulting increased cost of the product.

From *The Scotsman*, April 10, 1936. WJ Kinloch Anderson spoke about tailoring firms' problems.

Bespoke tailors are finding it more and more difficult to obtain suitable workmen – a representative of The Scotsman *was informed by Mr WJ Kinloch Anderson of Messrs, William Anderson & Sons, the Edinburgh firm of clothiers and outfitters. At one time, said Mr Kinloch Anderson, there were many tailors in the smaller towns employing an apprentice or two each. These apprentices tended to seek work in the larger towns once they became qualified. That was one of the most fruitful sources of fresh labour for the bigger tailoring firms in the larger towns. Owing to changed circumstances, a great number of tailors in the smaller towns are now taking their customers measurements and sending the material off to a factory in Leeds or London to be made up. Today there were comparatively few working tailors in the smaller towns as they could not exist owing to economic reasons.*

"Apart from the fact that there are now fewer opportunities for apprentices being trained," added Mr Kinloch Anderson, "there is the difficulty of getting boys to enter a long apprenticeship. Because of that, the average age of tailoring workmen must be a very high one, which is of course making the problem more serious."

The difficulty is not confined to Edinburgh. In London, which is of course noted for high-class tailoring, the shortage of suitable workmen has in recent years been so great that an application was made to the authorities and granted by them to allow skilled labour to be imported from foreign countries.

1942
▶ Introduction of soap rationing in the UK.
▶ Initial formation of the United Nations.
▶ Scheme for National Insurance devised by Lord William Beveridge (1879–1963).

1943
▶ US bombers make their first attack on Germany.
▶ The Royal Navy aircraft carrier HMS Dasher explodes and sinks off the Isle of Arran with the loss of 379 lives.

1944
▶ Pay as you earn, (PAYE) introduced in Britain by Sir Paul Chambers (1904–81) and Sir Cornelius Gregg (d.1959).
▶ Cancellation of the London Olympics.

1945
▶ The Red Army liberates Auschwitz.
▶ The bombing of Dresden.
▶ May: The war against Germany ends; Victory in Europe.
▶ August: A US atomic bomb devastates Hiroshima (Aug 6) and Nagasaki (Aug 9) in Japan. Unconditional surrender of Japan (Aug 14).
▶ October: The United Nations comes formally into existence (Oct 24).

103

The Second World War

The outbreak of the Second World War brought frightening and challenging times and significant hardship for the people of Britain. Kinloch Anderson had guidance and advice to share with their staff for their safety.

Edinburgh Evening News, Saturday October 7, 1939
"From Our Turret Window"

Since the last siren test in Edinburgh many more sirens have been added to the original complement, and it is considered that any air-raid warning will now be heard in every quarter of the city. Only in the event of a gas attack will rattles and hand bells be used by wardens. There seems to have been some doubt on this point, and the public should keep in mind that, if the enemy drop gas bombs, a warning to that effect will be given by wardens using rattles. The ringing of hand bells will indicate that the danger from gas poisoning has passed, and it is most important for the public to remember that, should gas bombs be dropped, the All Clear signal by the sirens does not mean that the city is free from the danger of gas. With regard to traffic during an air raid in the hours of darkness, the latest instruction is that all motor vehicles, unless engaged on some absolutely necessary work such as ARP (Air Raid Precautions), must quietly draw in to the side of the road and leave their sidelights on. If such vehicles were left at the roadside without any lights to indicate their position, the essential ARP services might be interfered with.

Air raids: "Do Not Rush"

Advice tendered by a Spaniard who experienced 400 air raids during the civil war was circulated to all members of his staff by Kinloch Anderson, JP, former City Treasurer and a past Master of the Edinburgh Merchant Company. Here are extracts from the sheet:

At the sound of the alarm, keep a cool head, follow instructions but above all, do not rush. Keep close to corners. Avoid being near doors and windows. If actual bombing finds you in the street go into nearest doorway and lie down flat close to the wall, with the head pointing inwards. If caught in the open lie in the lowest ground, and if there is grass or soft ground lie there. Bombs falling on soft ground sink in and the explosion is upwards.

If lying in the open cover your head with a folded coat or an open book to avoid injury from splinters from aircraft shells.

Left: Edinburgh's Princes Street Gardens were dug up, and air raid shelters were constructed in 1939.

Above: A pamphlet published by CJ Cousland & Sons Ltd showed the locations of Edinburgh's air raid shelters.

"Rubber is Handy"

What he regarded, from actual experience, as the most valuable advice was:

> *Carry a lead pencil or a piece of soft rubber or cork to put between your teeth to keep the mouth open. This avoids internal injury or the bursting of ear drums by concussion. It was only after painful experience that some of us during the last war stumbled on this precaution and it cannot be too often emphasised, that in an air raid one has to guard against panic inspired by the tremendous noise. The noise is very often out of all proportion to the direct effects of the bomb or shell – an encouraging fact that is worth keeping in mind – and so, if people are something in the nature of a terrible din and can remind themselves that the noise is frequently the worst part of it, then they will be able to keep cool heads. People who shout and run about in a panic are a menace to the community and in a time of stress can do much damage.*

Utility and Rationing

When the Second World War broke out in 1939, it had a bearing on how people dressed, both for work and for leisure. A national or global crisis of any kind always has serious implications for business and lifestyles, and no crisis is greater than the declaration of war. Money and goods became scarce. Everyday clothes had to be durable and practical. Clothes were rationed in Britain from June 1, 1941 and this continued until 1949, well after the end of the war. A utility clothing scheme was introduced by the government in 1942. Utility clothes were made from a limited range of quality-controlled fabrics marked CC41 (Civilian Clothing 1941).

Above: William Anderson & Son's *Outfitting for Men* catalogue 1940, produced just before clothes rationing began.

Below: The CC41 symbol found on utility clothes and furniture.

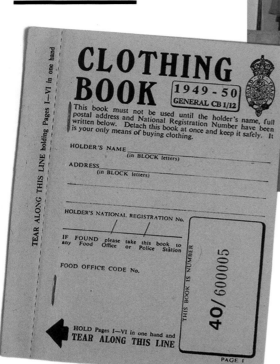

Above: A display of utility clothes designed by Norman Hartnell.

Left: A book of clothing coupons from the Second World War. Everyone was entitled to sixty-six clothing coupons per year. Children were allocated an extra ten coupons. Clothes for babies under four months, were exempt from rationing. The purchase of secondhand clothing was also exempt from rationing and so became very popular. Clothing rationing continued until 1952.

Until the utility scheme was introduced, the same number of coupons had to be surrendered for a named item of clothing regardless of the quality. The scheme aimed to provide price-regulated, better quality clothing and became known as "austerity regulations" – no more double-breasted suits, no extravagant lapels or trouser turn-ups, no more double cuffs on shirts. Trousers were held up with braces, and buttons replaced zips. Elastic for waistbands was not allowed other than for use in women's underwear.

Below: A government brochure with guidelines on how to *Make Do and Mend*.

Bottom left: It was possible to apply for supplementary clothing coupons if you had lost your belongings as a consequence of war damage to your home, or if you had been discharged from the army, or from hospital, or if you were on special leave from the forces.

Make Do and Mend

During the Second World War, fabric was essential for the war effort – such as uniforms and parachutes – and so civilian clothing was rationed.

Mending and repairing of clothing was encouraged by the government, as was as making new clothes, adapting old clothes, knitting and crocheting. Darning thread was not rationed and though some types of wool were available without rationing, people were encouraged to "unpick and knit again". People had to be very cautious about how they spent their very limited clothing coupons.

Clothing exchanges were set up by the Women's Voluntary Service (WVS). This was an essential service for parents struggling to find enough clothing for growing children.

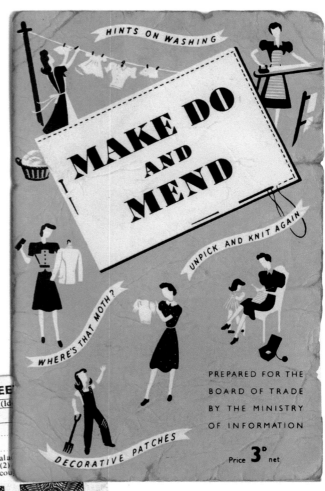

Retailers fought to keep their customers interested during the rationing period and William Anderson & Sons' catalogues showed their flexible and opportunistic approach. Clothing ranges included pyjamas, dressing gowns, underwear and "combinations", mufflers and other neckwear, handkerchiefs and gloves – and also a host of additional non-clothing items such as haversacks and kitbags, camp and field equipment, wardrobe and uniform trunks, attaché cases and suitcases, walking sticks, and boot and shoe racks.

Shortage of material was also a very definite worry, and by the end of the war people were understandably fed up with rationing, restrictions and the "Make Do and Mend" culture. Production of clothing then increased but mostly for export thanks to the "personal export scheme", whereby foreign visitors could buy clothing free of purchase tax.

This spread of illustrations: Retailers had to adapt and be flexible during times when there were material shortages. William Anderson & Sons also stocked ranges of underwear, pyjamas, walking sticks, shoe racks and ranges of handkerchiefs.

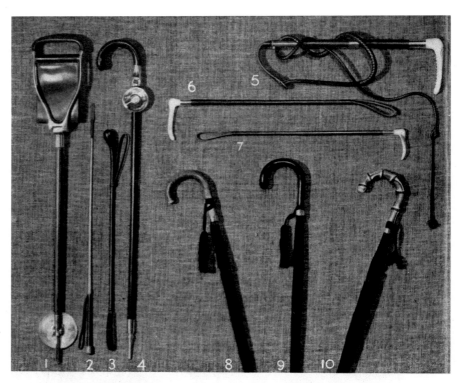

SEAT STICKS, CROPS AND UMBRELLAS

1946
▶ Introduction of bread rationing in the UK.
▶ Introduction of Family Allowance in the UK.
▶ Free milk in state schools in the UK.
▶ The BBC resumes broadcasting television.

1947
▶ The Edinburgh International Festival is founded.

1948
▶ Foundation of the National Health Service, the UK's healthcare system funded through general taxation.
▶ Bread rationing ends in the UK.

1949
▶ End of clothes rationing in the UK.
▶ Eire leaves the British Commonwealth.
▶ The setting up of NATO (North Atlantic Treaty Organisation).

1950
▶ A group of students from Glasgow University steal "The Stone of Destiny" from Westminster Abbey. (It is the stone over which, it is said, Scottish monarchs were crowned; stolen by King Edward I in 1296.)

1953
▶ The end of sweet and sugar rationing in the UK.

108

1963

▶ Dr Richard Beeching's report *The Reshaping of British Railways* has serious consequences for communities in Scotland. It leads directly to the closing of the Edinburgh to Carlisle route – the Waverley line. The towns of Hawick, Galashiels, Peebles, Melrose, Kelso, Penicuik and Gorebridge lose all their rail links.

1964

▶ Construction completed of Forth Road Bridge connecting Edinburgh to Fife.

▶ The Beatles come to the ABC Cinema in Lothian Road, Edinburgh.

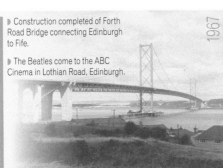

1967

▶ Oil companies start drilling in the North Sea.

1969

▶ The "Troubles" begin in Northern Ireland.

WJ Kinloch Anderson in the News

It can be clearly seen that Mr Kinloch Anderson was a leading spokesperson for the tailoring trade and that he attended meetings held all over Scotland. WJ Kinloch Anderson continued to be the "go to" authority on tartan matters.

> *The Linlithgow Gazette*, **September 16, 1949**
>
> *"Tailors had been rather surprised by the success of the personal export scheme," said Mr Kinloch Anderson and, "many Americans seemed to take 'terrific pride' in displaying a kilt made in Scotland." The scheme had been in operation for three years and had increased business by 10 to 15 per cent. There was demand from Scots in Canada, New Zealand, Australia and South Africa, as well as at home. Mr Kinloch Anderson gave this advice to fellow tailors: "Make the jackets and accessories smart but simple, and foster the use of Highland Dress as something that men of today will really want to wear frequently and not something to put on only for special occasions."*

The same philosophy is still applicable today!

Criticism of the government's new Price Control Order came from Mr Kinloch Anderson when he was representing the Scottish Merchant Tailors in Aberdeen in 1947:

> *The Aberdeen Press and Journal*, **October 1947**
>
> *"The Order gave the biggest profits to the lowest type of tailor. The high-class tailor got a moderate profit and the middle-class tailor got practically no profit at all." This Order was based on a maximum of 110 per cent increase over 1936 prices, so an 11-year span.*

In addition, there was concern over rising wool prices:

> *The Dundee Evening Telegraph*, **October 12, 1950**
>
> *"The average firm was still selling suits at the same price as they were six months ago," said Mr Kinloch Anderson. Most tailors had been laying aside cloth and were doing their best to maintain prices at a reasonable level but what was going to happen in nine months' to a year's time was anybody's guess.*

Above: A ladies pleated tartan skirt for outdoor wear, from a promotional company leaflet.

Purchase tax was a significant issue for the tailoring trade. It had been initiated during wartime as a means of directing consumption and raising revenue. "Utility" goods were exempt from it, while it stood at 100 per cent on luxury goods. Critics claimed that this unfairly penalised quality goods and badly affected exports. A resolution protesting against purchase tax was passed at the annual general meeting of the Scottish Federation of Merchant Tailors in Aberdeen. Mr Kinloch gave five reasons why it should go:

Aberdeen Evening Express, **October 17, 1951**

> *Why purchase tax should go:*
> *Its high level put bespoke tailors' prices outside the reach of some of the public. It affected the export trade – no firm can exist on export alone. It stopped recruitment to the trade. It made the gap between utility and non-utility too big. If the tax was abolished, loss to the Treasury would be comparatively small and could be made up in a better and healthier way.*

Bespoke tailors from all over Britain united to condemn purchase tax and the National Federation of Merchant Tailors, at their first ever joint conference in Edinburgh, unanimously agreed that purchase tax was a menace to craftsmanship and should be abolished.

Sometimes Mr Kinloch Anderson's articles provoked comment and discussion, as reported in a humorous column in a local paper:

Montrose, Arbroath & Brechin Review, and Forfar & Kincardineshire Advertiser **– Friday May 13, 1949**
Here and There, by J Scriblerus – "Women and the Kilt"

> *Reading an article by Mr WJ Kinloch Anderson on "Wearing Highland Dress", I was brought to a halt by this sentence: "Children below the age of four or five are generally not quite the right shape for the kilt, but from five onwards as a practical, economical and pleasing dress it is hard to beat." I was not for a moment disposed to doubt the truth of this statement, for Mr Kinloch Anderson is master of his subject, holding the Royal Warrant of Appointment as Tailor and Kiltmaker to HM the King, but I was troubled because I simply could not remember the typical shape of a four- or five-year-old. And the point was obviously an important one, or he wouldn't have mentioned it.*
>
> *The latter part of the article dealt with the controversial subject that history provides no authority for the wearing of the kilt proper by women, but admits that they have long worn tartan in other forms. "Whilst women dressed in male Highland Dress are occasionally seen... the adaptations of the dress for feminine use are appropriately becoming and exceedingly attractive."*
>
> *For outdoor wear, ladies, you may adopt the kilted tartan skirt or a tartan skirt with box pleats or inverted pleats. The jacket, if worn, should be of a cut-away style in tweed to tone or contrast. For evening functions, such as Highland Balls, where the men are in Highland Dress, tartan skirts are seldom worn, but tartan silk sashes fastened at the shoulder by a miniature plaid brooch are in order with the usual evening dress. It is greatly to be hoped that womenfolk will rest content with this very reasonable ruling and, having long since borrowed our trouser, will at least leave us in undisputed possession of our kilts.*
>
> *Gents are not given any advice by Mr Kinloch Anderson in this particular article, but the inference may be there all the same – like the four- and five-year-olds, they must take heed of their shape.*

Above: A child's version of Highland Dress, from a promotional company leaflet.

Kinloch Anderson Ltd

WJ Kinloch Anderson showed ceaseless dedication to his company. He was making strategic decisions for its future prosperity, not only at home but also overseas. In the post-war era, the company was supplying officers' uniforms for Scottish regiments in Canada and other Commonwealth countries.

Mr Kinloch Anderson went by ship on six-week trips to Canada in order to service their military and civilian needs. By so doing, he also received enquiries from shops in North America seeking supplies of tartans, tweeds and Scottish accessories.

So it was in the early 1950s, in order to respond to this opportunity and meet these export demands, that he set up Kinloch Anderson Ltd as a wholesale subsidiary company. He also acquired Conochie & Co Ltd (Clyde Street, Edinburgh, Union Street, Glasgow and Great Pulteney Street, London) who were wholesalers of a wide range of tartan merchandise items, including bonnets, scarves, sashes and travel rugs.

The McEwen Anderson Group of Companies 1966–1978

In the year of 1868, in the same year that William Anderson founded his business in Edinburgh, James McEwen formed a drapery business in Perth. Perhaps we should remind ourselves that at this time the American Civil War had only been finished for three years, and it would be another twenty years before the invention of the internal combustion engine.

As a 1968 brochure comments: "The world has changed considerably since then but today, over 100 years later, those two businesses have expanded, merged and become one of the largest family-owned retail groups of companies in Scotland, as well as being manufacturers of quality leisure and sportswear."

The story of McEwen Anderson is one of steady development through those years, with McEwens of Perth becoming one of the best known retail stores in Scotland, and William Anderson one of the finest men's tailoring and out-fitting companies in Britain, world-famous for its specialist Highland Dress department. Both businesses moved with the times and, in 1966, Alexander James Watt, Chairman of McEwens, and William James Kinloch Anderson, Chairman of William Anderson & Sons, realised their long-standing friend-ship both in and out of business had paved the way for further expansion with the merger of the two family concerns.

Over the years, the McEwens of Perth store progressively broadened its scope by adding new departments and became universally recognised as one of

1967

▸ Scottish football. April: England and Scotland play at Wembley. Scotland win 3–2 and are known as the "Wembley Wizards".

May: Celtic beat Inter Milan 2–1 to become the first British team to win the European Cup. Rangers play Bayern Munich in the final of the European Cup Winners Cup, losing 1–0.

1968

▸ The General Assembly of the Church of Scotland allows the ordination of women ministers.

1969

▸ Concorde, the world's first supersonic airliner, makes its maiden flight.

1970

▸ Commonwealth Games held in Scotland for the first time, in Edinburgh.

Left: The Tartan and Highland Dress department of the George Street premises in the 1950s.

Left: The Menswear department of the George Street premises in the 1950s.

1971
▶ The United Kingdom introduces a decimalised currency.

▶ Foundation of the 7:84 Theatre Company.

1973
▶ The United Kingdom joins the European Economic Community, the Common Market.

▶ November: The Miners' Strike. Prime Minister Heath imposes three-day working week.

1975
▶ Referendum on Common Market membership. "Stay in the EEC" won with 67% of the vote.

1978
▶ Launch of BBC Radio Scotland.

▶ Louise Brown becomes the first human in history to be born via in vitro fertilisation.

▶ "Winter of Discontent". Largest strike action since the General Strike.

Right: Grantown-on-Spey was founded as a planned settlement by Sir James Grant, the local landowner, in 1765. It is situated beside the River Spey at the northern edge of the Cairngorm mountains and, at the time of founding, was well served by two military roads. It was originally just Grantown after Sir James Grant but the "on Spey" was added in the late 1890s.

At one point, two railways reached Grantown-on-Spey which gave the town a boost to industry and tourism. Although both lines have since closed, the town is still a very popular tourist destination. The Strathspey Steam Railway has its current terminus at Broomhill Station, about three miles south of Grantown-on-Spey. It is hoped that in the future the line can, again, be extended to Grantown-on-Spey.

Right: Kingussie is a small town found in the upper Spey Valley of Badenoch and Strathspey. The name comes from the Gaelic "Ceann a' Ghiuthsaich" which means "head of the pine forest". The original settlement, surrounded by a pine forest, was created a Burgh of Barony in 1464. It was redesigned as a planned village by the Duke of Gordon in 1799.

Tourism and local business were given a boost with the coming of the railway in the 1860s and a golf course was opened in 1890. The Camanachd Association, which governs shinty in Scotland, was formed in Kingussie in 1893.

The Country Shop at Grantown on Spey

The Country Shop at Kingussie

Below: An example of a Kinloch Anderson sporran.

the finest ladies' fashion stores in Scotland. McEwens was a household name, synonymous with quality and service in Perth, the county of Perthshire and beyond. McEwens had bought Frasers of Perth who had Country Shops. The McEwen Anderson Country Shops, later to be renamed Kinloch Anderson Country Shops, ranged over the major tourist areas of Scotland and offered the best in Scottish craftsmanship as well as quality knitwear, tartan and tweeds. The shops were situated in the Cairngorm area at Aviemore, Grantown-on-Spey and Kingussie, also to the north at Dornoch in the Highlands, and at Ballater on Deeside. There were shops in the Perthshire towns of Crieff, Doune, Pitlochry and at Scotland's home of golf, St Andrews.

Greensmith Downes, another long-established family business, was brought into the McEwen Anderson Group of companies. It was situated at the other end of George Street to William Anderson & Sons and had a high reputation at the time as one of Scotland's foremost ladies' fashion shops, specialising

Old Edinburgh Name Revived

There was opened in Princes Street yesterday "The Luckenbooth," a shop for home and overseas visitors. Long ago luckenbooth was the name given to premises in the "Royal Mile," adjoining St Giles' Cathedral. "lucken" — meaning locked or closed—being used to distinguish the booths or shops from the open booths which lined other parts of the street. The new venture, sponsored jointly by William Anderson & Sons Ltd., and Turnbull & Wilson Ltd., has an attractive display of Scottish woven tartans, kilts, rugs and ties, Scottish jewellery (including a selection of the famous Luckenbooth brooches), Border knitwear, and table linens.

In this "News" photo are Mr J. M. Dick (Turnbull & Wilson), Mr W. Kinloch Anderson, Mrs Wilson (Turnbull & Wilson), and Mr H. G. Lindley, manager.

Left: The Luckenbooth gift shop, was first located in Princes Street.

Below: It moved to the Royal Mile where it was situated on the ground floor of the House of John Knox, the renowned Scottish reformer.

This was renamed as a Kinloch Anderson shop when the company name was changed, and the shop remained there until early in the 1990s.

Below: A Luckenbooth is a Scots word for a lockable stall or workshop. It is also a 17th-century heart-shaped symbol of love, traditionally given as a token of betrothal.

Detail: A company brochure from the 1960s.

in elegant clothes from the finest London and European fashion houses. Anderson's also ran The Luckenbooth shop in Princes Street, Edinburgh, catering for the many thousands of visitors who came to Scotland. After a number of years, The Luckenbooth moved to the historic Royal Mile where it was situated on the ground floor of the House of John Knox, the renowned Scottish reformer. This was renamed as a Kinloch Anderson shop when the company name was changed and the shop remained there until early in the 1990s.

In addition to Anderson's indispensable retail contribution to the group, Kinloch Anderson was the main manufacturing arm, building up its enviable reputation in the ladies' fashion field with the manufacture of tartan and tweed clothing in finest quality Scottish wool fabrics. A further manufacturing addition came with the acquisition of the small leather working business of Nicoll Brothers in Bankfoot, Perthshire. Nicoll Brothers was primarily known for its production of unique sporrans – without which no Highland Dress is complete – and also made handbags and other craft items in leather and deerskin.

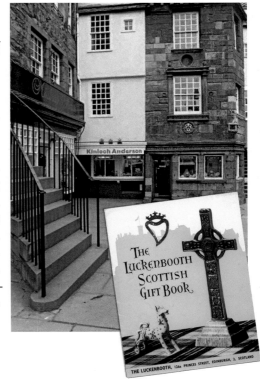

115

Celebration of the 100th Anniversary of William Anderson & Sons Ltd

Centenary Celebrations

The year 1968 was a special one for Anderson's. The company was celebrating 100 years and five generations of successful trading as tailors and outfitters. 100 years of consistency and success had come from hard work and forward thinking, together with the loyalty of long-serving staff, reciprocated by the company's loyalty to them. In celebration and thanks, a Centenary Dinner was held on October 28 1968 at the Adam Rooms of the George Hotel, George Street, Edinburgh, directly opposite the shop. Staff and colleagues from present and past were invited to the celebrations, as well as friends and business people from all over the country. *The Scotsman* pointed out in an article commemorating the company's centenary that Anderson's of George Street may have been 100 years old but it had a very modern approach to trading and a 100-year legacy of good customer service.

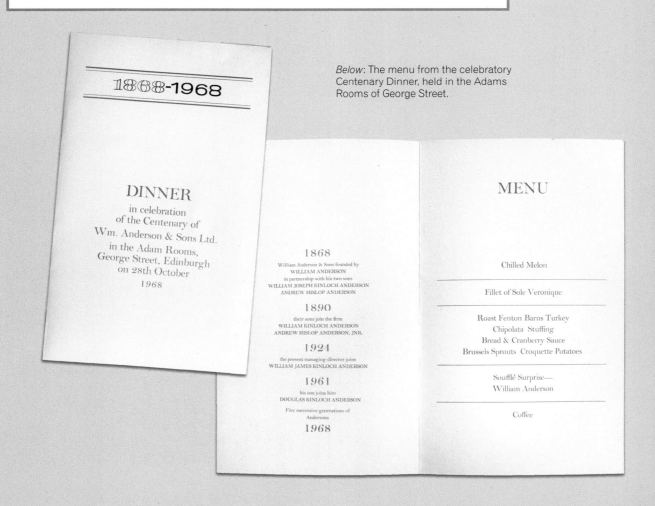

Below: The menu from the celebratory Centenary Dinner, held in the Adams Rooms of George Street.

1868-1968

DINNER
in celebration
of the Centenary of
Wm. Anderson & Sons Ltd.
in the Adam Rooms,
George Street, Edinburgh
on 28th October
1968

1868
William Anderson & Sons founded by
WILLIAM ANDERSON
in partnership with his two sons
WILLIAM JOSEPH KINLOCH ANDERSON
ANDREW HISLOP ANDERSON

1890
their sons join the firm
WILLIAM KINLOCH ANDERSON
ANDREW HISLOP ANDERSON, JNR.

1924
the present managing director joins
WILLIAM JAMES KINLOCH ANDERSON

1961
his son joins him
DOUGLAS KINLOCH ANDERSON

Five successive generations of
Andersons
1968

MENU

Chilled Melon

Fillet of Sole Veronique

Roast Fenton Barns Turkey
Chipolata Stuffing
Bread & Cranberry Sauce
Brussels Sprouts Croquette Potatoes

Soufflé Surprise—
William Anderson

Coffee

POST OFFICE TELEGRAM

Prefix. Time handed in. Office of Origin and Service Instructions. Words.

HD78 2.55 BUCKINGHAM PALACE OHMS 46

THE MANGING DIRECTOR WILLIAM ANDERSON AND SONS

GEORGE STREET EDINBURGH =

PLEASE CONVEY TO THE DIRECTORS AND STAFF OF

WILLIAM ANDERSON AND SONS ASSEMBLED FOR THEIR

CENTENARY THE SINCERE THANKS OF THE QUEEN FOR

THEIR KIND MESSAGE OF LOYAL GREETINGS

For free repetition of doubtful words telephone "TELEGRAMS ENQUIRY" or call, with this form at office of delivery. Other enquiries should be accompanied by this form and, if...

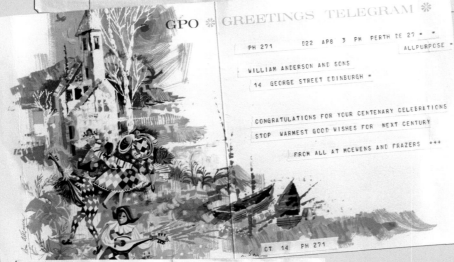

GPO ✳ GREETINGS TELEGRAM ✳

PH 271   D22   AP8 3 PM PERTH DE 27 =   ALLPURPOSE

WILLIAM ANDERSON AND SONS

14 GEORGE STREET EDINBURGH =

CONGRATULATIONS FOR YOUR CENTENARY CELEBRATIONS

STOP   WARMEST GOOD WISHES FOR NEXT CENTURY

FROM ALL AT MCEWENS AND FRAZERS +++

CT 14 PH 271

GPO ⬤ GREETINGS TELEGRAM

V 86 GTG 4.30 EDINBURGH TELEX 31/32 GREETINGS

WILLIAM ANDERSON AND SONS CO

ADAM ROOMS GEORGE ST EDINBURGH =

HEARTIEST CONGRATULATIONS ON YOUR CENTENARY

MAY YOUR NEXT HUNDRED YEARS BE AS SUCCESSFUL

= PORTER AND HARDING AND GEORGE HARRISON AND COY +

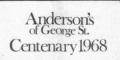

Presentation half the selling art

Five generations shaped firm

Right and pages 118–121:
October 24, 1968:
Scotsman articles about
the William Anderson
& Sons Centenary
Celebrations.

Anderson's of George Street Centenary, 1968

The Scotsman, October 24, 1968
Five Generations Shaped Firm – *By Joyce Dunford*

Proud though he is that his family firm, William Anderson & Sons, of George Street, Edinburgh, celebrates its centenary this year, with five generations of Anderson's having shaped it, Mr Kinloch Anderson, its managing director, is infinitely more interested in its future 100 years than its past.

"We like to feel we have deep roots," he said, "and that the thumbprint of Anderson's really means something, but we would very much dislike being considered a museum piece. We have always been progressive, never content to live on our history."

Nevertheless, for this birthday occasion he was ready to take time off from his preoccupation with the present and future to talk of some of the highlights in the firm's development.

The changes in costume have, after all, long been one of the most fascinating guides to social history, and, over the years, Anderson's has reflected a change in Edinburgh's way of life.

Mr Anderson showed me the sheets of parchment, covered with copperplate – lawyers knew nothing of typewriters then – on which his great grandfather William Anderson, had signed his partnership agreement when he started a company in 1868, in association with his two sons, William and Andrew, at the shop where the George Hotel now is, just opposite the present premises.

A tailoring business only at the time, it was conducted in a very hushed manner behind darkened windows, with no question of any show of what was available within, and only heavy bolts of cloth to be seen inside – a far cry from today's display of goods which gets you inside the shop almost before you realise you are there.

William Anderson died in 1880, leaving his two sons to manage the firm, and after three years they moved to the other side of the street, where the shop now is, to allow for expansion.

They were reinforced in 1890 by each of their sons joining the firm straight from school – William Kinloch, father of the present managing director, and Andrew Hislop.

By a coincidence, both the older men died in 1903, leaving two sons, then 23 years old, to run the business. They were full of bright ideas.

Soon after they took over they acquired a second shop next door and started selling ties – an unheard of innovation for a tailor's at that time – and in 1912 they gave the firm an extra status by changing from a partnership to a limited company.

With the war imminent, the military uniform side of the business was enormously important. Army uniforms were then extremely elaborate, and each officer had to have a considerable number. The two Anderson brothers introduced another extension to their sales – the supplying of all army accoutrements. Including Sam Browne belts and topees for service in India. It proved an immediate success."

"After the 1914–18 war, my father

also started making and selling ready-to-wear suits," Mr Anderson said. "Again, complete heresy then, but something which later many others copied and which is now a very important part of our business."

Following those same forward-looking ideas, Mr William Anderson was also wholly in favour of his son going to Edinburgh University to take a Bachelor of Commerce degree, and then to London to gain further business experience, before entering the firm. "But I was in and out of the place from the age of seventeen onwards – always during my vacations." He was made a director in 1930.

When the Second World War broke out in 1939, Anderson's was still very much in the uniform business and became the meeting place of many an Allied officer, particularly Canadians stationed here.

While they were ordering their uniform they noticed the tartan goods by which Anderson's had by then become famous – they were given the Royal Warrant as kiltmakers in 1935. Several of the Canadians had some Scottish connections and were eager to trace their family tartans and to buy the host of Scottish goods made with them.

"This was the beginning of the enormous export trade we have now developed all over the world, but particularly in Canada and America," Mr Anderson said. "When the Canadians returned home they kept sending for more and more tartan goods for themselves and their friends."

So constant was the demand that, armed with a list of all those who have

been in touch with the firm, he went to Canada in 1948 on a one-man trade mission. His visit was a great success and was the basis of the sizeable business in Canada and America which they now have. It was into the export side of the firm that Mr Anderson's son Douglas came in 1960, after taking an economics degree at St Andrews University, and he is now a director of the separate wholesale company which runs it. He spends several months in the year visiting customers all over the world and often sponsors exhibits at trade fairs abroad.

Up to the last war, the atmosphere at Anderson's was rather like that of a discreet men's club, with only male assistants. During the war, with so many of the staff joining at the services, it was necessary to introduce women assistants, and from then it was a short step to catering for the women's trade.

"We began by making women's tartan skirts, to complement the men's kilts and then it seemed obvious to sell the knitwear to match," Mr Anderson explained.

"We are still primarily a man's shop, and men can buy here everything they need, literally from top to toe, but the women's end, though much expanded from at the beginning, is intended to be specifically leisure wear."

What did he think of the future in menswear would be? I asked him. "There is certainly a movement towards brighter clothes," he said, "and to rather more simplified garments. But changes in the men's sphere are very gentle, and apt to go round in cycles, an extra fullness in the jacket, or slightly narrower trousers, that sort of thing."

Anderson's of George Street Centenary, 1968

The Scotsman, October 24, 1968
Presentation Half the Selling Art – *By Joyce Dunford*

The successful modern businessman knows that the presentation of his goods is half the art of selling. So it was no surprise to see the attractive special centenary décor which Anderson's George Street windows have been given.

Inside it is one of those shops where you can wander round admiring the clothes instead of having to ask for them to be dragged out of drawers and boxes. Mr HG Lindley, the manager and a director, said the choice at Anderson's of materials for custom-made suits or the ready-to-wear kind was very wide.

There were all the classic styles, and exceptional ones for specialist needs. The range of tweed jackets alone numbers 400, with almost as many pairs of trousers to go with them and styles to appeal to a father or son.

Scottish tweeds, Cheviots, Yorkshire cloths – Anderson's stock them all. The only criterion they have is that the quality should be the best.

Ready-to-wear suits are apparently as popular as the made-to-measure these days – it is just a question of how much a man wishes to spend, and the same man will often have both in his wardrobe.

Men go to the rear of Anderson's to choose their suits, in quiet comfort – there is a most effective three-dimensional picture on the end wall showing Edinburgh as it was when the firm was founded. They are likely to find themselves buying shirts and ties to match their suits on the way out, for these are attractively displayed.

A whole range of shirts are hung in special Cellophane coverings – easily seen through – dozens of them on a rack and in every size. Large proportions are of the drip-dry variety, and Anderson's find that pure white ones are about equal in popularity with coloured stripes.

Near the shirts, is a sock and tie bar, where again it is a matter of minutes to find something to go beautifully with the shirt, and how very much simpler it makes the whole business of shopping.

Anderson's also stock men's underwear, which has received very much the same new look and presentation as the shirts, and having chosen underwear and socks, it is a short step to selecting a new pair of shoes, since there is a special shoe department.

After that perhaps the owner of the new suit will feel he might as well have a Burberry or coat to go over it. If so there is a host from which to choose, some with lovely scarlet linings, others more restrained.

Highland Dress has always been a great speciality there – boys going at an early age to be fitted with a first kilt and paying return visits over the years.

One of several displays in the shop shows a man wearing an impeccably tailored kilt and jacket, with his wife in a long tartan evening skirt to match, a little boy completing the family circle in a miniature version of his father's outfit.

The wife, incidentally, has borrowed her blouse motif from the male Highland Dress shirt, complete with ruffles.

Anderson's send their Highland Dress outfits all over the world and they can be seen on many a St Andrews night gathering.

It was the tremendous experience they had of supplying tartan in all its forms which helped them to develop their tourist trade, particularly at Festival time.

Businessmen sometimes decry the festival, but they have found it brings them a large number of customers from abroad, many of whom remain as mail order customers.

It was chiefly because of this link that Anderson's developed their Scottish gift department. They deprecate the word "souvenir", so apt to betoken shoddy material, but they sell Scottish glass, pottery and jewellery, Scottish maps and books, horn spoons and a variety of attractive things made from deerskin.

In the women's department there is a great emphasis on co-related colour schemes. Jumpers and cardigans are specially knitted for Anderson's in the Shetlands and there are lambswools and cashmeres of every colour in the rainbow, teamed with coats and tweed skirts.

Mother-and-daughter outfits, especially liked by Americans, can be bought there, too, and reversible capes, tartan one side, plain the other.

The mixing and matching to be done there was endless. If you wished, you could wear a cape, hat, skirt and handbag all in the same tartan or tweed without looking the least over-dressed.

Another item in this department which seemed an excellent idea, was a see-through pack containing a skirt length with a side zipper to match. It was not surprising to hear these are highly popular as gifts.

There is nothing at all in Anderson's to suggest 100 years of age, except perhaps that one intangible – an awareness by the staff of a reputation to live up to and of the tradition of the service they inherited.

Did men buy more clothes these days than they did?

"A greater number of men are certainly buying more, a result, I suppose, of the affluent society. Not, of course," he added rather quizzically, "as much as the women are buying, but after all we must go some way towards trying to keep up with them."

Keeping up in every way with fashion and modern sales techniques is obviously what he intends to do at Anderson's.

In the 1970s, as the Kinloch Anderson business expanded strongly into clothing manufacturing and overseas sales, its compatibility with the retail activities of the McEwen Anderson Group diminished. Ultimately, in 1978, it was mutually and amicably agreed that McEwens of Perth should revert to being an independent company and that Kinloch Anderson should continue its development separately. In due course, this decision proved to be the right one for both parties.

It is commonly recognised that many family CEOs never retire. Mr Kinloch Anderson took great care to plan his retirement but not before he had written some guidance and detailed advice to Douglas for the future direction of the company. His wife, too, had ideas for his retirement away from the business to Boat-of-Garten in Inverness-shire where he was honorary treasurer and then president of the Golf Club. From time to time he wrote in the columns of the local newspaper, *The Strathspey Herald*, and drew attention to the danger which the sparks from the engines of the Strathspey steam train posed to his own and neighbouring gardens along its route! He never lost interest in the company and remained on the company board for meetings, discussion and policy making. The company is indebted to his wisdom, intelligence and good leadership.

> WJ Kinloch Anderson, former chairman and managing director, Kinloch Anderson Ltd.
>
> Born May 19, 1907. Died August 5, 1997.

Right: The Kinloch Anderson immediate family group in 1911, with young Kinloch (front row, end right); Kinloch's sister Elsa (front row, end left); Kinloch's father, William (far left); Kinloch's mother Eliza, (back row, with large hat); and Kinloch's grandmother, (centre, holding the baby).

Chapter Six

DOUGLAS
KINLOCH ANDERSON

FIFTH GENERATION

KINLOCH ANDERSON
HOUSE TARTAN

DOUGLAS Kinloch Anderson was born at the beginning of the Second World War. Food was rationed and luxuries were scarce. He clearly remembers the first time his father returned from America and brought back a piece of chewing gum, which he cut into several small segments and shared with his friends! Douglas went to George Watson's College where his talents were both academic, sporting and occasionally playing in the second violins of the school orchestra. After his MA honours degree in Political Economy and Geography at St Andrews University he followed with a postgraduate course in business studies at Edinburgh University. He gained practical retail store experience in Marshall Fields of Chicago, and then in Harrods of London, training for his future business career.

When Douglas joined his family company in 1960 he was soon to be given the responsibility of developing the wholesale company whilst his father continued to run the retail side.

However, prior to this, he was involved with the Country Shops which belonged to the jointly owned McEwen Anderson Group. There were many of these shops throughout Scotland and, reflecting on this, he says, "The concept was actually ahead of its time."

These shops were merchandised at the top-of-the-range quality level and needed both local and tourist customers in order to thrive. However, the Scottish tourist industry then was a fraction of what it is now, and activities such as skiing at Aviemore were very basic, as were most golfing facilities and other visitor attractions. Scotland welcomed around five million visitors

Page 123 and above: The Kinloch Anderson House tartan creates a simple, stylish and easy-to-wear image. The soft cream and brown colours are uncomplicated, navy maintains a link to the Kinloch Anderson tartan, and pale gold identifies with the Kinloch Anderson brand logo.

Opposite: Douglas Kinloch Anderson.

Below: Scotland House, based in Virginia, specialised in British and Scottish merchandise and was staffed and managed by Kinloch Anderson for over a decade.

Scotland House

"The Bonniest Shop in America"

GIFTS *and*
Wearing Apparel
from SCOTLAND
ENGLAND & IRELAND

607 SOUTH WASHINGTON ST.
ALEXANDRIA, VIRGINIA
22313

703 - TE. 6-8855

Opposite page: (Top right) A Kinloch Anderson promotional leaflet.
(Bottom left) Promotional photography featuring Kinloch Anderson ladies skirts.

EVENTS IN THE TIME
OF DOUGLAS KINLOCH
ANDERSON

Statement by WJ Kinloch Anderson to the 50th Annual General Meeting of William Anderson & Sons Ltd, on Wednesday November 28, 1962

If I may be pardoned for finishing on a personal note I would like to say how much pleasure it gives me to have my son, Douglas, now established here with us. He is the fifth successive generation of Andersons in the business. If we go on for another six years the company will reach the venerable age of 100. It is nice to think that there is every prospect that the Andersons will still be well established when that milestone is reached. You will be asked later to approve the appointment of Mr Douglas Anderson as a director of the company.

and the industry was worth £1.6 billion. Today we have 15 million visitors and the industry is worth over £11 billion. Furthermore, Scottish tourism was essentially limited to the few summer months. There were no busloads of tourists and the rural roads in the Highlands were another limiting factor. It was many years before small shops in rural Scotland were in demand and this came from a middle- to lower-quality tourist market that evolved.

Douglas was always an eager traveller, and his broad, outward-looking approach greatly benefitted the Kinloch Anderson Company.

As soon as his father introduced him into the market in Canada and the USA, he quickly recognised its potential. At that time, Scottish clothing and accessories were in demand and were being imported into the best tourist shops in North America and Bermuda. The wholesale export of Kinloch Anderson skirts developed in parallel with this trading pattern. It was Douglas who masterminded the development of the Kinloch Anderson skirt production in Scotland with small factories in Glasgow, Tranent and Muirkirk and later the move to a large manufacturing base in Restalrig, Edinburgh in 1980.

As sales in the USA increased, a sales agent company, Wray & Turnbull, was appointed to further extend sales into retail outlets. Wray & Turnbull also represented other British clothing companies for the import of clothing, such as knitwear, tweeds, silk ties and duffle coats. It was based in Madison Avenue, New York and Douglas travelled frequently to the USA at this time.

1979
▶ Referendum on Scottish Devolution to create a Scottish Assembly wins a majority (turnout 63%) but fails to reach the threshold of 40% of the electorate.

▶ Margaret Thatcher (1925–2013) becomes first woman Prime Minister of the UK.

1980
▶ Ronald Reagan (1911–2004) elected US President.

▶ John Lennon (b.1940) assassinated.

1981
▶ President Reagan wounded in assassination attempt.

▶ Pope John Paul II (1920–2005) survives assassination.

▶ HRH Prince Charles (b.1948) marries Lady Diana Spencer (1961–97).

1982
▶ Princess Grace of Monaco (b.1929) killed in a car crash.

▶ Birth of Prince William.

▶ Argentina invades Falkland Islands.

▶ Visit of Pope John Paul II (1920–2005) to Britain.

Subsequently, Wray & Turnbull was acquired by Kinloch Anderson, along with one of the best retail customers, Scotland House in Alexandria, Virginia near Washington DC. Scotland House specialised in British and Scottish merchandise and was staffed and managed by Kinloch Anderson for over a decade.

However, the development of inexpensive clothing and knitwear coming into the USA market from Hong Kong and China was a revolution which fundamentally changed the pattern of trading in the American clothing and fashion industry.

A second Kinloch Anderson shop had been opened in a wealthy suburb of Washington, but the option to expand a chain of Kinloch Anderson shops in the US market was declined. In hindsight, this was the correct decision as, subsequently, small clothing shops in the USA gave way to the multiples.

"I've only got three minutes..."

Selling high quality ladies skirts in export markets was a competitive business and Douglas Kinloch Anderson recounts an experience early in his career, when he was, in his own words, "a very green and inexperienced salesman". Douglas had an appointment with Lord & Taylor, a prestigious upmarket New York department store.

"I took with me from Edinburgh a large case with samples of the skirt range. At the store on the day of the meeting, the merchandise manager breezed into the room and said, 'I've only got three minutes, show me the range.' I took a deep breath and with some trepidation replied, 'I have brought this range 3,000 miles especially to show you, and if you haven't got time to view it properly, I won't open the case.' There was a pregnant pause and the manager said, 'OK, Doug, let's do it!' Two hours later I left the store with what was the best skirt order I had ever written. If only every business meeting had such a happy outcome!"

1984
- The miners' strike is led by Arthur Scargill (b.1938). It lasts one year, is a time of great hardship for the miners and is ultimately unsuccessful in its aims.
- Discovery of the AIDS virus.

1985
- Mikhail Gorbachev (1931–99) is appointed leader of the Soviet Union.
- Live Aid: a concert to raise funds to fight famine in Ethiopia.
- Chris Bonington (b.1934) reaches the summit of Everest.
- Football: Heysel Stadium disaster.

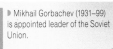

1986
- Edinburgh hosts the Commonwealth Games and incurs a £4 million deficit.
- Space shuttle Challenger explodes on take-off killing crew of seven.
- Chernobyl disaster: Russian nuclear reactor explodes (initially kills 31) and contaminates a huge area and its people with radiation.
- Appearance of Halley's Comet.
- Construction of the Channel Tunnel begins.

Scotland House

The city of Alexandria, Virginia has many connections with Scotland. For many emigrant Scots this east coast seaport on the southern bank of the Potomac was their first stepping stone to the new and promised land where they sought fame and fortune. Much of the character of the city has been preserved, and today, as well as being an elegant residential area close to Washington DC, it is one of the focal points for many thousands of tourists who go there every year to see the many charming 18th- and 19th-century buildings, and relive something of America's colonial past.

Scotland House was beautifully situated with its L-shaped building housing not only the Scottish wool garments for which Kinloch Anderson was renowned, but also some of the finest quality British and Scottish clothing, accessories and gifts to be found in North America.

A further development at Scotland House was the establishment of a wholesale warehouse to supply the needs of stores throughout the United States and in Bermuda.

NEWS RELEASE

Kinloch Anderson Ltd., the Scottish based business with sixteen stores and a ladies sportswear manufacturing company in Scotland, are pleased to announce a further development of their interests in the U.S.A., by the amalgamation of Wray & Turnbull, Ltd. with their U.S. company -- Kinloch Anderson of Scotland (USA) Ltd.

This amalgamation is concurrent with the retirement of Mr R.S.H. Turnbull, who for many years has been President of Wray & Turnbull Ltd. having had a long and close liaison with Kinloch Anderson Ltd., both through the wholesale selling and distribution of Kinloch Anderson products in the U.S.A., and through their joint association in running the retail store of Scotland House, in Alexandria, Virginia.

In the future there will be one company with a retail division and a wholesale division. The retail division, based in Alexandria will trade as Kinloch Anderson Ltd., Scotland House; the wholesale division will trade under two names -- Wray & Turnbull Ltd., and Kinloch Anderson of Scotland (U.S.A.) Ltd. The sales and marketing part of this wholesale division will operate from New York, whilst the importing, wholesaling and shipping parts will be based in Alexandria. There will be a joint office organization in Alexandria to serve both the wholesale and the retail divisions.

Douglas Kinloch Anderson, Kinloch Anderson Newsletter, 1977

Earlier this year, a letter from a customer of our USA shop was received in Edinburgh. It serves as a timely reminder of the ultimate objective and purpose of our work – to give good value and service and to satisfy each and every customer. This is the end product of every single person's work in this company, no matter whether your job is at a sewing machine or adding up figures in an office, or typing invoices, or packing parcels, or selling to customers in one of our retail shops, or any other of the dozens of different activities in Kinloch Anderson.

Alexandria, Virginia, USA
3rd January, 1977

Dear Sirs

This Christmas season I was somewhat incapacitated and found shopping for gifts rather difficult. I called your Alexandria store and your Mr Banks was not only most helpful, but kind and very understanding. Via telephone I was able to secure my husband's and godson's Christmas presents.

So much of life has become impersonal that when one encounters kindness and lovely service, one is obliged to take a moment and say thank you.

Sincerely,

Mrs Wingfield Roberts

Douglas Kinloch Anderson, Kinloch Anderson Newsletter, June 1979

Sometimes, if I look at all the processes involved in getting one of our products into the hands of a satisfied customer, it is a near miracle that anything is achieved. An order has to be obtained at the right time in some far-flung place and then processed here correctly. The design of the cloth and of the garment have to be right. The raw materials must be scheduled to arrive for production at the right moment. All the manufacturing processes have to be accurate. The invoicing and documentation has to be completed, and the packing and shipping arrangements must ensure that delivery is made on time. And then the customer has to pay – which sometimes can be a problem. And finally, the ultimate consumer in Paris or Rome, or Tokyo or Sydney, or Montreal or wherever, has to like the finished product, buy it and be satisfied with it.

Kinloch Anderson

Right: The company was making over 100,000 skirts a year, with agents all over Europe. Europe had become the biggest market and the demand was insatiable. The picture on the right is of Kinloch Anderson garments and accessories on sale in a Danish store. In 1979 Kinloch Anderson exports exceeded £1 million.

EVENTS IN THE TIME OF DOUGLAS KINLOCH ANDERSON

1987
- Princess Anne (b.1950) created Princess Royal.
- IRA bomb kills eleven at Remembrance Day ceremony in Enniskillen, Northern Ireland.
- Terry Waite (b.1939), special envoy of the Archbishop of Canterbury, is kidnapped in Beirut by Hezbollah.
- The ferry the Herald of Free Enterprise sinks killing 188.

1988
- George HW Bush (1924–2018) elected US President.
- Lockerbie disaster.
- Piper Alpha disaster.

1989
- Exxon Valdez spills cargo of oil in Alaska.
- Berlin Wall dismantled.
- Poll Tax (Community Charge) implemented in Scotland but not the rest of Britain. 20,000 protest.
- Hillsborough Stadium disaster.

1990
- Rugby Grand Slam for Scotland.
- Nelson Mandela (1918–2013) freed.
- Iraq invades Kuwait.
- West and East Germany reunited.
- Community charge implemented in England.
- John Major (b.1943) becomes UK Prime Minister.

Left: Kinloch Anderson kilts, bonnets, sporrans, scarves, pins and brooches promoted during "British Week" in Denmark.

Above: A page from a Kinloch Anderson wholesale catalogue showing a selection of scarves.

1991

▶ Gulf War begins.

▶ Prime Minister Rajiv Gandhi of India (b.1944) is assassinated.

▶ Violence escalates in Yugoslavia.

▶ Soviet Union comes to an end.

▶ Community Charge replaced by Council Tax.

▶ Last of Apartheid laws abolished in South Africa.

1992

▶ Race riots in Los Angeles following the beating of Rodney King by police.

▶ Bill Clinton (b.1946) elected US President.

▶ Prince Charles and Princess Diana announce their separation.

▶ Windsor Castle is badly damaged by fire.

▶ Privatisation of the coal industry.

1993

▶ Czechoslovakia is split into Slovakia and Czech Republic.

▶ Mass suicide at Branch Davidian cult headquarters in Waco, Texas.

▶ European Union Inaugurated.

▶ Buckingham Palace opened to the public.

▶ Sarajevo placed under UN rule.

Douglas Kinloch Anderson, Kinloch Anderson Newsletter, 1979

1979 will be remembered by us as the year in which we received the Queen's Award for Export Achievement, and this award has brought much pleasure and satisfaction to everyone in the company. We have set ourselves high standards for the 1980s, but I am confident that we will live up to them!

EⁱⁱR

The Master of the Household has received Her Majesty's command to invite

...... Mr. Neil Darling ......

to a Reception to be given at Buckingham Palace by The Queen and The Duke of Edinburgh for Winners of The Queen's Awards for Export and Technology in 1979 on Thursday, 14th February 1980 at 6 p.m.

The reply should be addressed to
The Master of the Household, Buckingham Palace
Guests are asked to arrive between 5. 30 p.m. and 6 p.m.   Dress: Lounge Suit

Above right: The invitation to a reception at Buckingham Palace, received by (Neil) Duncan Darling (pictured below). Duncan is Douglas's cousin who worked with Kinloch Anderson for 39 years.

Kinloch Anderson Newsletter, June 1980: Invitation to Buckingham Palace

At the end of January three very official regal looking envelopes dropped through the letterboxes. They were nothing to do with the Birthday Honours list but invitations to a reception at Buckingham Palace for Winners of last year's Queen's Award for Export & Technology. The three lucky recipients chosen to represent the company were Mr Douglas Kinloch Anderson, Mr Duncan Darling and Miss Laura Cowan (from the Muirkirk factory). They met Her Majesty The Queen, HRH The Duke of Edinburgh, HRH The Prince of Wales, HRH The Duke of Gloucester, The Lord Chamberlain and Chief of The Clan MacLean."

Duncan Darling is Douglas's cousin and he spent most of his working life with Kinloch Anderson. In 1973 he first worked in the cloth section at Rose Street (behind the George Street shop) and after training was appointed Purchasing Manager in 1976. Duncan was the Commercial Manager of the company when he retired 39 years later in 2012. His commitment and years of service to the company deserve to be recognised.

The Queen's Award for Export Achievement

In Scotland, the Kinloch Anderson manufacture of ladies tartan and tweed skirts continued to flourish, and in 1979 the company won the Queen's Award for Export. The company was making over 100,000 skirts a year, with agents in Italy, France, Germany, Austria, Switzerland, Denmark and Norway. Europe had become the biggest market and the demand was insatiable.

Above: The presentation of the Queen's Award for Export Achievement to Douglas Kinloch Anderson in 1979. Left to right: WJ Kinloch Anderson, Margaret Kinloch Anderson (Kinloch's wife), the Lord Provost Kenneth Borthwick, Douglas Kinloch Anderson, Deirdre Kinloch Anderson, Jane Johnson (Douglas's sister).

Right: The Queen's Award.

Extract from *The Scotsman*, Friday, March 2, 1979
£1 Million for Export
JOYCE DUNFORD TALKS TO DOUGLAS KINLOCH ANDERSON

The young can flirt with high fashion and low quality in their giddy teens but with the years comes the wisdom of buying less often, the best possible materials — natural fibres win hands down — well tailored and classic styles. This approach goes not only for the non-teenager in this country but all over Europe in North America and even in parts of the Far East, particularly Japan, where women's dress is almost entirely Westernised.

Which is why the firm of Kinloch Anderson, for over a century specialists and patterns and tweeds in Edinburgh in George Street, have now decided to put most of the efforts they had one time concentrated on selling clothes for the male, into manufacturing and marketing skirts and woollen coordinates for women.

When Kinloch Anderson celebrated their century ten years ago, Douglas Kinloch Anderson had already started in this field. Now managing director of the firm — the fifth generation in the family business — he has found this side of the company's activities growing rapidly in recent years. In the past year more than £1 million worth of their goods have been exported to Europe alone, and the American subsidiary company have been responsible for that same amount of dollars in the sale and distribution of Kinloch Anderson and other British-made textile products.

Kinloch Anderson's main factory and administrative base is in Edinburgh's Restalrig area, and they employ about 200 men and women there and in Tranent, Glasgow and Muirkirk.

"Most people in Edinburgh have little idea of the existence of the manufacturing side of Kinloch Anderson," he said "and we expected when we moved out of the retail side of the men's business, once our mainstream activity, they might think we had gone out of existence. Very much not so! Our export trade of women's clothes is substantial — well over the £1 million mark in Europe alone—and goes on increasing in many markets, particularly in the past five years."

He showed me with pride, a large album of coloured photographs taken of customer's shops around the world. It's one of his hobbies, and Hamburg, Vienna, Copenhagen, Rome, Brussels, Amsterdam and New York were a few of the many cities of which he had a record.

He regards Kinloch Anderson as a specialist business, personally developed through the direct contacts of its four directors and many sales agents, which he leads. "We are fiercely independent, feeling we would lose our identity, and that personal touch, if we merged with any of the large groups." As with Colin Hutcheson, he speaks French and German, and spends many weeks each year travelling to meet and talk to customers around the world.

Left: Douglas Kinloch Anderson, pictured with his son Peter and his wife Deirdre, at Buckingham Palace where he received his OBE for Services to Export, in 1983.

Douglas Kinloch Anderson Receives an OBE

In 1983, Douglas received an OBE for Services to Export.

He had been prepared to invest in the global market by attending trade shows in Europe, North America and the Far East. This commitment to his marketing strategy resulted in significant growth of overseas sales.

Douglas masterminded the manufacturing, marketing and export of Kinloch Anderson's skirts and coordinated knitwear, from the company headquarters in Restalrig, Edinburgh and also from factories in Tranent and Muirkirk.

Left: Douglas in the Restalrig factory displaying Anderson Tartan fabric.

Ladies Skirts

Douglas used the best photographers and models in order to promote the excellence of the finest quality garments made by the company. We are still proud of these images to this day.

Ladies skirts: Douglas attended trade shows in Europe and also invested in the highest quality photography to promote the excellence of the merchandise.

Tailored for Scotland

Ladies skirts: Douglas decided to put the efforts they had at one time concentrated on selling menswear, into manufacturing and marketing skirts and coordinates for women.

138

Above: A Kinloch Anderson Licencees conference held in Tokyo, June 2008.

Below: A Kinloch Anderson reception held at the British Embassy in Tokyo in June 2006. Guests included Kinloch Anderson Managing Agents Hideo Achiwa, Japan (back row, seventh from right), Doosik Yi, South Korea (back row, third from right) and Carl Shieh, Taiwan resident (back row second from right).

The Far East

World recession slowed the growth and potential for the development of garment manufacturing in the UK and exporting overseas. Kinloch Anderson prices were relatively high and there were changes away from classic fashion. People were no longer buying "clothes to last a lifetime". However, Douglas's travels had taken him to Japan where he saw the development of licensee partnerships being made by top quality clothing companies. So, he took up the challenge to develop the Kinloch Anderson brand of merchandise "under licence" in Asia.

Once again, the leadership decision was ahead of its time with the development of the Kinloch Anderson brand. Douglas recalls the early days. "One of the markets was Japan, and I went there in 1972 to find a sales agent."

He saw that other foreign brands, like Burberry or Ralph Lauren from America, who had built up their business by exporting, were starting to look for partners who would make their products under licence in their own home country and for sale in that market. With all its heritage and Scottish authenticity, Kinloch Anderson could do likewise. Production costs in Europe and America were rising, and this was an alternative solution.

"My contact in Japan was Hiro Ikeda, a really nice man who had a postgraduate degree from Cambridge, so he was pretty much bilingual. He introduced me to Fukusuke. It started in a small way. They were major producers of the ladies footwear worn with the kimono called the 'tabi' but they had a huge range of textile products."

The initial agreement with Fukusuke was not in the clothing area as he had expected, but with beautiful china tableware – clothing came later. The Chairman of Fukusuke, Mr Tsujimoto, made a visit to Scotland and painted a picture of the Forth Bridge. "He was a very keen amateur artist and he gave me one of his paintings," said Douglas.

Left: Douglas shares a toast with the Chairman of Fukusuke, Mr Tsujimoto.

By 2020, Douglas reckoned he had been to Japan more than 125 times – an average of three times a year since 1972.

His way of building a global business was to go out and meet the people, make the contacts, understand their culture and find out if there was a gap in the marketplace that the company could fill. A classic example of this was when he was contacted by an agent in Italy who was looking to replace a shoe brand that had been discontinued in South Korea. Douglas was off to Italy two days later and shortly thereafter on the plane to Seoul. He made a licence agreement that produced a great outcome!

"Undoubtedly the most successful of all our licence agreements has been in South Korea with a family-owned and family-managed company who design and manufacture the finest menswear clothing, both for formal and informal wear," said Douglas. Kinloch Anderson shops were established in many of the best department stores in South Korea as well as in iconic shopping malls. The brand's market cover was increased by extending it into three ranges, each attracting a different age range and type of customer: Kinloch Anderson, Kinloch by Kinloch Anderson and Kinloch2. The intention for the future is to widen the sales of these ranges into similar markets in other countries.

International Brand Partnerships

The development of the Kinloch Anderson brand name in overseas markets, particularly in Asia, will undoubtedly be one of Douglas's legacies and, to this day, International Brand Partnerships make an important contribution to the success of the company.

When Douglas embarked on this future potential for Kinloch Anderson, brand development was in its infancy; he was very much a pioneer in this field. Many people may not fully comprehend how this type of business takes place.

Working with overseas companies at a local level requires considerable knowledge of the country and its culture and for Douglas that always meant actually going to that country in person.

Initially, direct agreements were made with compatible companies who had the ability to manufacture high quality products for their market under the Kinloch Anderson brand name.

The establishment of support from the Kinloch Anderson design team was important, together with imported products from Scotland. These companies were also required to have the right marketing connections to establish and to run the Kinloch Anderson retail outlets, either independently or as concessions in department stores.

By 2019, there were over 300 such Kinloch Anderson shops in the Far East. The companies must share in the success or otherwise of the relationship – a genuine partnership. However, as with all contracts, there were many formalities and safeguards to be included and arrangements to be confirmed before going into the market. These usually related to advertising and promotional activity and the interpretation of the Kinloch Anderson brand identity.

Anti-clockwise from the left: A selection of Kinloch Anderson products made under licence overseas, including, childrenswear, young ladieswear household textiles and babywear.

Above: A Kinloch Anderson menswear shop in South Korea.

Kinloch Anderson took up the challenge of working in China, with a view to benefiting from the unparalleled potential of this huge and expanding market. The company was not the first one to encounter difficulties with agreements made in China. Chinese culture is different in so many ways and the business "playing field" is equally different. For the Chinese, "loss of face" is something to be avoided. When difficulties arise, one way to bypass this is to appoint a Chinese "negotiator" who can help to bridge the gaps and smooth the path of co-operation. It is definitely who you know more than what you know that matters most in China. Without having lived in China, or acquired an understanding of the languages (or languages), communication can require the assistance of translators, and without in-depth knowledge of the matters under discussion, this can also be somewhat unreliable.

The company's first agreement was made through an introduction made by an existing Kinloch Anderson Agent. It was with a very large and successful luggage company who supplied a significant percentage of the Chinese market. They had distribution contacts for entry into the best Chinese stores and wanted to diversify, beginning with menswear but aiming eventually to

EVENTS IN THE TIME OF
DOUGLAS KINLOCH
ANDERSON

1994

▶ Nelson Mandela becomes first black president of South Africa.

▶ IRA announces ceasefire in Northern Ireland.

▶ Channel Tunnel opens.

1995

▶ Tall Ships Race, Leith. Kinloch Anderson design the Leith tartan and make a kilt for the skipper of the Jean de la Lune, which led the Parade of Sail and came in at 10th place.

▶ Oklahoma bombing.

▶ Nerve gas attack on Tokyo subway.

▶ Japanese city of Kobe hit by earthquake, killing 5000 people.

▶ End of the Bosnian War.

1996

▶ The Stone of Destiny is permanently returned to Scotland, to be housed in Edinburgh Castle.

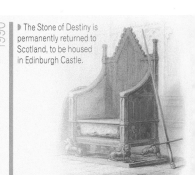

Left: A dinner held for Kinloch Anderson's partners, Taipei, 2004.

cover as many categories of merchandise as they could. They opened a few Kinloch Anderson menswear shops but found the clothing market a greater challenge than they had anticipated. Some mistakes were made in the appointment of personnel and sub-licensees and a further complication was the pirating of the name "Kinloch 1868". Ultimately, the positive outcome achieved by the negotiator for Kinloch Anderson was the introduction to the Chairman of one of China's biggest and best manufacturers of men's underwear based in Qindao. There are now over 100 shops in Chinese department stores under the Kinloch Anderson name in men's underwear!

The Kinloch Anderson licence business in Taiwan came about through Douglas's participation in a trade mission, as a result of which he met an agent for Kinloch Anderson. With a population of 23 million, it is quite a compact market and today, with fifteen different licensee companies, Kinloch Anderson has made a considerable impact on the marketplace – with menswear, ladieswear, childrenswear, leather goods, men's shirts, shoes, household textiles, accessories and gift items. Kinloch Anderson shops can be found on several different floors in one department store in Taipei!

1997
▶ Scots-born Tony Blair (b.1953), former pupil of Sir Eric Anderson (1936–2020), becomes UK Prime Minister.

▶ Referendum on Scottish Devolution. The result is Yes–Yes to devolved powers and tax-varying powers.

▶ Diana, Princess of Wales, dies in a car crash in Paris.

1998
▶ Impeachment of US President Bill Clinton. (He is acquitted of the charges in February 1999.)

1999
▶ A Scottish Parliament sits for the first time in 272 years. Donald Dewar (1937–2000) is elected as First Minister.

Above: "I can't believe it. I was in Taipei and what did I see – a Kinloch Anderson bus!"

Douglas says, "Our licensees come together as a kind of Kinloch Anderson family usually twice a year, and they do joint advertising on the Taipei buses. I remember the Lord Provost of Edinburgh, after he had visited Taipei, he phoned me and said, "I can't believe it. I was in Taipei and what did I see? A Kinloch Anderson bus!"

On the importance of politeness
Douglas recalls: *In the 1980s I was in Japan with the Chairman of the Scottish Tourist Board. One of my long-standing Japanese business associates invited us to dinner at an extremely sophisticated traditional Japanese restaurant in Tokyo. After fifteen or so elegant dishes had been served, the host announced that the next dish was a very special turtle soup, which indicated that the meal was coming to its conclusion. However, this was followed by the serving in beautifully hand-painted china beakers of what looked like red wine.*
"This is the greatest delicacy of all", said the host.
"May I ask what it is?" asked the Chairman politely.
"Turtle's blood!" was the reply.
Ashen-faced he turned to me. "What shall we do?"
I replied, "We have come to represent Scotland – we drink it!"

Japan
Doing business in Japan is very different. You never meet a Japanese business person one-to-one. They always meet you as a group and are extremely polite. Meetings usually start with them doing their best to hold the conversation in English. Sooner or later discussion develops and they start talking to each other in Japanese. Douglas thought it would be a good idea to learn a few phrases in Japanese – things like, "Oh, what a good idea, I think we should pursue it." He tried it and of course it stopped everything immediately! It is also impossible to know whether a meeting has gone well or not.

However, one of the good things about working in Japan is that when they do decide, they keep to their word.

The Shanghai–Maglev train

This was quite an uncanny experience. The speed of the train was shown at the end of the carriage and went up to 250 mph (max speed 267 mph). The train was so silent and so smooth. It was uncanny, and as you looked out of the window at the cars travelling along the open roads, they seemed to be "crawling"!

Above: The high-speed Shanghai–Maglev train.

An unforgettable experience

I recall one unforgettable experience when I was asked to spend a night with my then Japanese agent and his wife at their country house. This house was situated on a small island south of Osaka and must have been a beautiful retreat in the summer. However, unfortunately it was mid-winter and the paper walls of the house offered no protection from the sub-zero temperature outside. Trying to sleep on the bare floor with nothing but a single blanket and a wooden pillow was undoubtedly more difficult for me than for him! He was not only resilient physically but also unbelievably strong mentally. He once told me that he had spent two weeks in a Shinto Monastery, during which time he had not uttered a single word and had spent all day sitting against a wall meditating.

Wako department store, Tokyo

The strong connection with Japan continued with the company's 150th Anniversary celebrations in 2018. A Kinloch Anderson Exhibition was held for one week on the exhibition floor of the renowned Wako store in the Ginza district of Tokyo.

Below, left: The Kinloch Anderson 150th Anniversary Exhibition in Japan.

Below right: The Wako Co. Ltd. building where the Kinloch Anderson Exhibition was held.

Above: The interior of Kinloch Anderson's shop in Leith.

Below: Kinloch Anderson's headquarters in Restalrig where manufacturing took place between 1980 and 1990.

Leith and Restalrig

Under Douglas's management, the company developed its four divisions: retail, wholesale and corporate, production, and brand development. Things never stand still on the retail side, and it was in Douglas's time that the cost of running the George Street shop became unrealistic. The shop was sold in 1980 and the Kinloch Anderson headquarters moved to Restalrig. For a few years Kinloch Anderson retail customers either came to the shop in the High Street at John Knox House or to a small unit in the same building at Restalrig where the clothing manufacture was taking place.

Then another move was made in 1990, this time to Leith. Part of the retail shop was a joint venture with Johnston's of Elgin, selling Johnston's finest knitwear alongside Kinloch Anderson's Highland Dress, complemented by the Kinloch Anderson Heritage Room museum. Johnston's at Kinloch Anderson was essentially a shop full of finest woollens at "outlet" prices for tourist groups travelling around Scotland.

Unfortunately, the prices were competing with similar Johnston's knitwear selling in the city centre, so its future potential had to be cut short. The knitwear was briefly replaced by Bryant of Scotland, before the shop refocussed and returned to be fully stocked and managed by Kinloch Anderson.

The popularity of kiltwear was experiencing an upturn. For many decades, the kilt had been mostly worn for church on Sundays and by country gentlemen, it was little seen in the cities and even less so south of the border. However, this was changing quite rapidly. The kilt was becoming increasingly

Above: The Shore, Leith.

Below: The Caledonian Club in London.

popular as fine attire for weddings, for special formal occasions and also by young people for informal wear at sporting events.

Kinloch Anderson was ideally placed to respond to the new demand and furthermore, a Highland Dress Service was initiated at the Caledonian Club in London. The Caledonian Club was founded in 1891 as a private members' club – located at 9 Halkin Street, SW1, near Belgravia – and with the intention to become the headquarters for Scotsmen in London. Over the years, the club has successfully developed and extended its premises and activities, including opening full membership to women in 2010 and anyone of any country in 2011. It has many societies for members to join and is a fine venue for dinners, celebrations and events. The Kinloch Anderson Highland Dress Service is given both to club members and club visitors. Initially it was once a month, but this has recently increased and now also includes weekends.

The choice of location for the Kinloch Anderson shop in Leith was a calculated risk. Leith was little developed at the time. However, the spacious shop was impressive and provided a relaxed atmosphere in which staff could give customers their best service and advice, and the Heritage Room afforded a viewing window onto the Kinloch Anderson kiltmaking production unit. There was also the customer convenience of ample private parking and a frequent bus service from the city centre.

An important addition to these attributes has been Leith's successful bid to be the final resting place of the *Royal Yacht Britannia*.

The *Royal Yacht Britannia*

The year 1990, when Kinloch Anderson moved to Leith, was actually the time when Deirdre was given her first job in the company. It was part time and she was responsible for delivering the "Johnston's at Kinloch Anderson" leaflets to the tourist trade.

In her role as "the Leaflet Delivery Girl", Deirdre came into contact with very many people in the hotel and tourist industry. Just eight years later she became the President of the Leith Chamber of Commerce.

When she was Vice President in 1997 it was the time when Forth Ports were bidding for the Scottish Parliament (which they lost) and for the *Royal Yacht Britannia* (which they won).

Terry Smith, CEO of Forth Ports said to her: "Deirdre, if we get the *Royal Yacht Britannia* for Leith, you can hold your President's Reception next year on board." So they did, and she did! A Leith President had never had so many people wanting to come to their reception, but she had no illusions as to why they wanted to come – and it was not to listen to her!

Leith President's Reception – *Royal Yacht Britannia* – Wednesday October 14, 1998.

Excerpts from the President's welcome speech:

> *This is probably the best attended reception that a Leith President has ever had. The great attraction of this wonderful yacht has existed for a very long time. When* Britannia *was in California as part of the Queen's State Visit to the West Coast of the United States, the President of one of the largest US aviation companies was invited with his wife to attend a government seminar on board* Britannia.

Above: Deirdre Kinloch Anderson.

Above: Standing, front to back – Eric Milligan, (Lord Provost of Edinburgh 1996–2003), Deirdre Kinloch Anderson, Douglas Kinloch Anderson, Sir Jack Shaw.

This was part of the "Sea Days" scheme, whereby a government department took over Britannia for a day and invited prominent figures from the worlds of commerce and industry to attend a seminar on board. On this occasion, the company President was not particularly enthusiastic, but when his wife saw the invitation, she made sure they accepted "because there was no way she was going to miss coming on board the Royal Yacht and seeing where the Queen lives". There may be some similarities with this evening.

During her forty-three years of life as a Royal Yacht, kings, queens, presidents and prime ministers have been entertained on board. On her decks, knighthoods have been given and marriage bans have been read. Built as a floating home for the Queen and her family, she has been used throughout the world for state visits, official banquets and receptions, royal honeymoons and annual summer cruises. She saw action in Aden in 1986 and

countless important business seminars have taken place on board. Britannia was perhaps a luxury, but she was a practical solution to some of the Queen's more difficult visits. She provided accommodation without risk and a base for reciprocal hospitality. The yacht belonged to the dignity and status of our Queen's lifestyle and, perhaps most important of all, it was a place where she could relax.

The City of Edinburgh, and Leith in particular, now has one of the great sea treasures of the world. I believe that Leith has become the yacht's final resting place because Forth Ports understand ships and shipping to the very core, and here she will be looked after and cared for just as she always was. Now, instead of sailing the world, the world will come to Britannia.

It was to be twenty-one years later that Deirdre's son John followed in his mother's footsteps as President of the Leith Chamber of Commerce – but his was a more modest introduction!

A Man of Vision

As the fifth generation of management of the company, Douglas Kinloch Anderson has been a man of vision and determination, believing in the diplomacy of leadership, with designation of responsibility to others and allowing himself to find time for social and professional contributions outside the company's more routine demands. Indeed, he has followed in his ancestor's footsteps in this regard. Douglas was President of the Edinburgh Chamber of Commerce, a Board Member of the Scottish Tourist Board, Moderator of the Leith High Constables and, like his grandfather, Master of the Merchant Company of the City of Edinburgh. All this was a platform for recognition of his business experience and knowledge such that he was invited to serve on the boards of a number of investment trusts run by Martin Currie, Fidelity, and Foreign & Colonial. His other significant interest has been with the Royal Warrant Holders Association, of which he was the National President in 1994, and he has remained on the council, thereafter, travelling from Scotland to attend meetings in London.

Taken from Douglas's speech at presentation of Queen's Award for Export, June 12, 1979:

"I used to be fond of telling people that I represent the fifth generation of the Anderson family, adding, that of course the generations degenerate – this remark being made in confident anticipation of a chorus of denials. However, this merry quip has, on occasion been met with an embarrassed silence, so I have rather backed off this approach and now concentrate on the true facts, which are that this company is very much alive and exporting because of the hard work, the cooperation and the dedicated efforts of everyone employed in Kinloch Anderson."

By Appointment to
Her Majesty The Queen
Tailors and Kiltmakers
Kinloch Anderson Ltd

By Appointment to
HRH The Duke of Edinburgh
Tailors and Kiltmakers
Kinloch Anderson Ltd

By Appointment to
HRH The Prince of Wales
Tailors and Kiltmakers
Kinloch Anderson Ltd

Kinloch Anderson
SCOTLAND

Tailors and Kiltmakers, Tartan and Highland Dress since 1868

Chapter Seven
BY ROYAL APPOINTMENT

OVER the years, Kinloch Anderson has received many accolades, but particular pride is taken in the Royal Warrants of Appointment as Tailors and Kiltmakers to HM The Queen, HRH The Duke of Edinburgh and HRH The Prince of Wales.

The concept of the Royal Warrant of Appointment dates back to the advent of the monarchy. By the fifteenth century, royal tradesmen were appointed formally in writing by means of a Royal Warrant issued by the Lord Chamberlain, a practice which continues to this day. The Royal Warrant has always been a recognition of personal service of the highest order.

It is granted to a named individual within the company who is then responsible for ensuring that the warrant is correctly used. In order to be considered for the granting of a Royal Warrant of Appointment, a company must provide the member of the Royal Family concerned, or their household, with products or services in significant quantity over a period of time.

The final decision to grant a Royal Warrant of Appointment is made by the member of the Royal Family concerned.

The company first supplied HM King Edward VII in 1903, but the first Royal Warrant was granted by HM King George V in 1934, and another thereafter by HM King George VI. Kinloch Anderson has held a Royal Warrant of Appointment as Tailors and Kiltmakers to Her Majesty The Queen since 1955, His Royal Highness The Duke of Edinburgh since 1956, and His Royal Highness The Prince of Wales since 1980.

Page 153 and swatch above: The thistle is the oldest recorded national flower of Scotland and is used as a key trademark for Kinloch Anderson, Scotland. The Kinloch Anderson Thistle tartan incorporates the rich, deep purple, green and black colours of the Scottish thistle with a blue and burgundy overcheck.

Below: William Anderson & Sons first became suppliers to King Edward VII (1841–1910) in 1903.

Above: The George Street shop in 1960, showing the Royal Warrants of Appointment to HM The Queen and HRH The Duke of Edinburgh.

Below: The first Royal Warrant, granted by HM King George V (1865–1936).

Right: A William Anderson & Sons leaflet from 1934 referring to the first Royal Warrant.

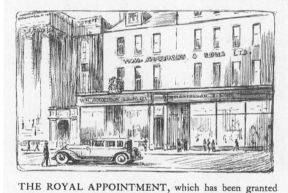

Tailors by Appointment to H.M. The King

WM. ANDERSON & SONS, LᵀᴰG.

Highland Dress Tailors and Outfitters

14-16 GEORGE STREET, EDINBURGH, 2

And at 155 HOPE STREET, GLASGOW, C.2

Telegraphic Address: "Uniforms, Edinburgh"

THE ROYAL APPOINTMENT, which has been granted as Tailors to H.M. The King, is a gracious and formal recognition of standards of quality and workmanship which had long won the practical approval of discerning customers. . . . It is also more than this ; just as a military decoration is a matter for pride not only to the individual who receives it, but to the whole unit to which he belongs, so is this Royal act a welcome recognition of the standards of George Street, which the firm of William Anderson & Sons have always striven to uphold.

WM. ANDERSON & SONS LTD.

TAILORS BY APPOINTMENT TO H.M. KING GEORGE V

14 to 16 GEORGE STREET, EDINBURGH 2

157 HOPE STREET . . GLASGOW, C2

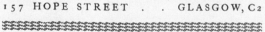

The Royal Warrants and the Royal Warrant Holders Association

As a result of being honoured with three Royal Warrants of Appointment as Tailors and Kiltmakers, the Kinloch Anderson Company has a long connection with the Royal Warrant Holders Association (RWHA). This originated in 1840 when a gathering of "Her Majesty's Tradesmen" held a celebration of Queen Victoria's birthday and formed themselves into the "Royal Tradesmen Association". Subsequently this became the Royal Warrant Holders Association, which in 1907 was recognised by a Royal Charter of Incorporation which was renewed in 2007.

All companies which hold a Royal Warrant may join the association, and nearly all of them choose to do so. There are currently some 800 such members, holding one, two or three Royal Warrants. One of the most important aims of the association is to provide the best possible liaison for members with the Royal Household and those responsible for running it. This takes place through the Lord Chamberlain's Office. A Royal Warrant of Appointment is given to an individual grantee, as the representative of the company concerned, and that person is responsible for maintaining the highest levels of service and the excellence of their products. Adherence to the Lord Chamberlain's rules is an important part of this responsibility.

The RWHA is a very active organisation, based in London at 1 Buckingham Place, with the Secretary and CEO leading a small dedicated team. The Council is composed of Grantees, one of whom is elected as President each year. Nowadays the Council is supported by an Executive Committee, whose

Above: The logo of the Royal Warrant Holders Association (RWHA).

Left: National President of the Royal Warrant Holders Association, Alec McQuinn (far left), pictured wearing Kinloch Anderson Highland Dress at the Edinburgh Royal Warrant Holders Association Dinner, Edinburgh, 2012.

Above: The Annual Banquet of the Royal Warrant Holders Association at Grosvenor House, 2019.

membership is largely comprised of the office bearers: the Chairman of the Executive committee, the President, the Vice President, the Past President, the Honorary Treasurer, and the Chairmen of the two main charitable bodies, the Charity Fund and the Queen Elizabeth Scholarship Trust (QEST).

There are five local associations, in Windsor, Aberdeen, Edinburgh, Sandringham and Highgrove, all locations where the Royal Family have residences. These associations are greatly involved in local activities for members, as well as participating in the many events run by the national association. Sporting events include golf, tennis, shooting and fishing. Recent seminar meetings have included guidance on the archiving of historical information and the important matter of sustainability.

Two of the major social events of the RWHA each year are the Annual Luncheon and the Annual Banquet. Douglas Kinloch Anderson, having earlier been the President of the Edinburgh Royal Warrant Holders Association, became the national President in 1994. HRH The Princess Royal was the guest of honour at the Luncheon that year.

Douglas recalls that prior to the Annual Banquet that year it had been suggested at a Council meeting that Kinloch Anderson should design a special RWHA tartan, and the Grantee of the home textiles and wallpaper company, Sanderson, offered to print the tartan on a tablecloth for the long top table.

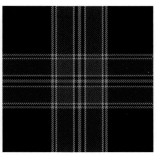

Above: The Royal Warrant Holders Association tartan designed by Kinloch Anderson in 1994 when Douglas Kinloch Anderson was President of the Association.

Left: Douglas Kinloch Anderson, the President of the Royal Warrant Holders Association, making a speech at the 1994 RWHA Annual Luncheon.

Seated, left side of photograph: Mr Barry Reed of Austin Reed; HRH Princess Anne, The Princess Royal. Seated on the right, the Lord Mayor of London, Sir Paul Newell.

This was duly done, and at the same time a table napkin in the tartan was made for each of the 1200 guests. Following the main speech, which had been delivered by Douglas's brother Eric, then Headmaster of Eton College, Douglas addressed the guests and was able to say, "As always, of course, you should leave all the cutlery on the table, but on this occasion you are most welcome to take away your tartan napkin!"

Charitable involvement has long been an important part of the association's role. The members' Charity Fund dates back to 1902 and supports the charitable activities of member companies, often with the involvement of some of their employees. The fund's mission is to support local charities thereby "making a difference where it matters".

Left: HRH The Prince of Wales visits the Sandringham RWHA marquee at the Sandringham Flower Show, 2012.

Above: The QEST alumni group photo at Saddlers Hall, London, for the launch of the QEST book *A Celebration of British Craftsmanship*.

In 1990, to mark the 150th anniversary of the RWHA and the 90th birthday of HM Queen Elizabeth, The Queen Mother, the association established the Queen Elizabeth Scholarship Trust (QEST) for the further advancement in the United Kingdom of modern and traditional crafts and trades. Scholarships are granted to individuals to develop their talents as armourers, basket makers, lot printers, ceramicists, calligraphers, silversmiths, charcoal burners, milliners, stone cutters, wood workers, weavers and many other skills. QEST has developed hugely and since its inception has supported over 500 scholars and apprentices. The trust was recently honoured by HRH The Prince of Wales becoming its patron.

One of the unique and most enjoyable aspects of the RWHA is the diverse nature of the members, who represent a complete cross section of occupations and lifestyles. Whether the member companies are single-ownership or large corporate entities, all members share a common belief in the excellence of their product or services. Contacts are therefore made between members who might otherwise never have known each other, and many lasting friendships have been formed.

1901 — Death of Queen Victoria, Queen of the United Kingdom of Great Britain and Ireland, Empress of India (1819–1901).

1903 — William Anderson & Sons supplies tartan to HM King Edward VII (1841–1910).

1934 — William Anderson & Sons' first Royal Warrant is granted by HM King George V (1865–1936).

Queen Victoria and Tartan

Just as King George IV's visit was pivotal in the story of tartan, Queen Victoria was to bring her own influence to bear in the continuing popularity of tartan and Highland Dress.

Victoria was proclaimed sovereign at St James's Palace, on June 21, 1837, and Edinburgh heard the news on June 24. The Queen was crowned on June 28, 1838 at Westminster Abbey, and the City of Edinburgh celebrated with a public banquet, a display of fireworks and a bonfire on Arthur's Seat.

In 1842 the Queen and Prince Albert made their first visit to Scotland. The young Victoria was hugely excited by Sir Walter Scott's novels and was keen to explore her northern kingdom, which, after the purchase of Balmoral, some years later, was to become a regular and favourite destination.

Her Majesty arrived in the Firth of Forth on Wednesday, August 31, landing at Granton next morning, earlier than expected, and drove through the city to Dalkeith Palace. Lord Provost Forrest and Council Members were not at the city boundary as planned to receive Her Majesty and present the keys to the city. This episode quickly became the subject of a ballad, "Hey, Jamie Forrest, are ye waukin' yet?"

Arrangements were made for Saturday, September 3, when the Queen made up for having disappointed the people, entering the city in state, driving up the High Street, greeted by huge crowds. At the Royal Exchange (now the City Chambers) by the site of the Mercat Cross, the Lord Provost presented the keys, before the Queen continued to the Castle. The procession left for Dalmeny Park, by the Mound, Princes Street and the Dean Bridge.

Below: Queen Victoria and her husband Prince Albert made their first visit to Scotland in 1842. Scotland was later to become a favourite and regular destination.

1936

▶ William Anderson & Sons' second Royal Warrant is granted by HM King George VI (1895–1952).

1955

▶ Kinloch Anderson is granted a Royal Warrant by Her Majesty Queen Elizabeth II (b.1926).

1956

▶ Kinloch Anderson is granted a Royal Warrant by His Royal Highness Prince Philip, The Duke of Edinburgh (b.1921).

1980

▶ Kinloch Anderson is granted a Royal Warrant by His Royal Highness Prince Charles, The Prince of Wales (b.1948).

Above: Queen Victoria and Prince Albert fell in love with the Highlands and purchased Balmoral Castle.

On Monday, September 5, the royal party drove through the city to Queensferry, then crossed to Fife and drove north.

Queen Victoria and Prince Albert fell in love with the Highlands and purchased Balmoral in 1848, and the land surrounding it in 1852. A new castle was built – commenced in 1853, completed in 1856 – and it has been the Scottish home of the Royal Family ever since.

At Balmoral, Prince Albert personally took care of the interior design, where he made great use of tartan. He utilised the red Royal Stewart and the green Hunting Stewart tartans for carpets, while using the Dress Stewart for curtains and upholstery. The Queen designed the Victoria tartan, and Prince Albert designed the Balmoral tartan which remains the exclusive tartan of the Sovereign of the United Kingdom.

To this day, the Kinloch Anderson Company is privileged to hold the Balmoral tartan for the Royal Family and has tailored garments in it over many years. The Balmoral tartan is the private property of the Royal Family and its use is restricted to family members who have been granted permission from the Sovereign.

Balmoral *Victoria* *Royal Stewart* *Hunting Stewart* *Dress Stewart*

Victoria and Albert spent a considerable amount of time at their estate and, in doing so, hosted many "Highland" activities. Victoria was attended by pipers, and her children and staff were attired in Highland Dress. Prince Albert himself loved watching the Highland games. Regrettably, at the same time as these fashions swept over Scotland, the Highland population suffered grievously from the Highland Clearances, when thousands of Gaelic-speaking Scots from the Highlands and Isles were evicted by landlords to make way for sheep; in many cases the landlords were the very men who would have been their own clan chiefs.

Above: "The Drawing Room" (1857). A watercolour by James Roberts (c.1800–1867). An interior view of the drawing room of Balmoral Castle. The billiard room can be seen through the open door. The carpets are Royal Stewart tartan. The chairs and curtains are Dress Stewart tartan.

The Balmoral Tartan

The Balmoral tartan was designed by Queen Victoria's husband Prince Albert in 1857 and, while predominantly grey with overchecks of red and black, the background contains a thread of black and white yarns twisted together to achieve the appearance of the rough-hewn granite so familiar in Royal Deeside. It is worn by HM The Queen and several members of the Royal Family but only with the Queen's permission. The only other approved wearer of the Balmoral tartan is the Queen's personal piper. (The Estate workers and Ghillies wear the Balmoral tweed.)

Based on ideas considered when the Balmoral tartan was designed, short lengths have been woven with a blue overcheck and a green overcheck, with the latter being made into a jacket for the HRH The Prince of Wales.

Below left: HRH Prince Charles, The Prince of Wales and HRH The Duchess of Cornwall wearing the Balmoral tartan.

Below right: Her Majesty Queen Elizabeth II and HRH Prince Philip, The Duke of Edinburgh pictured in the grounds of Balmoral Castle.

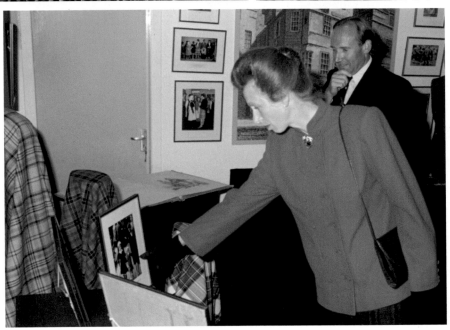

Above: This picture shows the different weights of Balmoral tartan fabric which Kinloch Anderson hold for use by the Royal Family. The Balmoral tartan design has an unusual marled grey twisted yarn which reflects the colours of the granite of the Balmoral Estate.

Top right: HRH The Prince of Wales wearing a jacket from Kinloch Anderson in Balmoral tartan with a green overcheck.

Right: Visit of HRH The Princess Royal to the Kinloch Anderson factory and headquarters at Restalrig, Edinburgh in 1988. Balmoral tartan (draped left) is held by Kinloch Anderson for use by the Royal Family.

Photographs Displayed in the Kinloch Anderson Heritage Room Museum, at their Premises in Leith

Left: HRH Prince Charles, The Prince of Wales wearing a Royal Stewart tartan kilt, and HRH The Duchess of Cornwall wearing a Lord of the Isles tartan silk skirt. The eldest male child of the reigning Scottish monarch is designated The Lord of the Isles, and the alternative Scottish titles for His Royal Highness and his wife are Duke and Duchess of Rothesay.

Below left: HM The Queen and HRH Prince Philip at the Royal Scottish Pipers Society Centenary Ball at the Assembly Rooms, Edinburgh, June 1982. Prince Philip is wearing a Royal Stewart tartan kilt and Her Majesty is wearing a Dress Stewart tartan sash.

Above: HM Queen Elizabeth pictured in Deeside, wearing a pleated skirt in Old Stewart tartan.

Below right: Prince Edward, The Duke of Windsor, wearing the Balmoral tartan.

Above: Pictured at Balmoral, 1999: (Left to right) Prince Andrew, The Earl of Inverness; Prince Charles, The Duke of Rothesay; Prince Harry; Prince Edward, The Earl of Strathmore; Princess Anne, The Princess Royal; Prince William; Zara Phillips; Princess Beatrice; Princess Eugenie; Prince Philip, The Duke of Edinburgh; HM Queen Elizabeth II.

Above: HRH Princess Anne wearing an Ancient Hunting Stewart tartan skirt, young Zara Phillips wearing a Balmoral tartan skirt, and young Mark Phillips wearing an Ancient Hunting Stewart tartan kilt.

Below: HRH Prince Edward, The Earl of Wessex; and HRH Sophie, The Countess of Wessex. Their alternative Scottish titles are The Earl and Countess of Strathmore.

Above: The Royal Family on a Royal Visit to Edinburgh in July 1979. HRH Prince Charles, The Prince of Wales, is wearing Dress Stewart tartan, and HRH Prince Philip, The Duke of Edinburgh is wearing a Royal Stewart tartan kilt.

Below: Full dress is worn with the Royal Stewart kilt and fly plaid, Balmoral headwear with a feather plume, Royal Stewart handknitted hose and black buckle brogue shoes. The jacket is a No 1 dress jacket made in black barathea with a black velvet collar and gold insignia on the right-hand sleeve (detail below, left). The piper pictured is Alistair Cuthbertson who was the Sovereign's Piper from 2006–2008.

The Sovereign's Piper

The "Piper to the Sovereign" is a position held by a serving Pipe Major (Warrant Officer) in the British Army who is responsible for playing the bagpipes at Her Majesty The Queen's request. He also acts as an honorary Page of the Presence within the Royal Household.

The position was established in 1843. A year earlier, when Queen Victoria and Prince Albert visited the Marquess of Breadalbane at Taymouth Castle, they discovered the Marquess had her own personal piper. The Queen was taken with the idea of having one for herself, writing to her mother, the Dowager Duchess of Kent:

> "We have heard nothing but bagpipes since we have been in the beautiful Highlands and I have become so fond of it that I mean to have a Piper, who can if you like it, pipe every night at Frogmore."

The office has been held continuously since then (apart from a brief interruption, 1941–1945 during the Second World War).

The Sovereign's Piper's Uniforms

The Sovereign's Piper fulfils the greatest majority of his duties in the four royal residences of Buckingham Palace, Windsor Castle, the Palace of Holyroodhouse and Balmoral Castle. The uniforms of the Sovereign's Piper are made by Kinloch Anderson. He wears "working dress" or "No 1 full dress" depending on the occasion, and his kilts are made in the Royal Stewart tartan, the Ancient Hunting Stewart tartan and the Balmoral tartan.

Left: A detail of the gold insignia on the right-hand sleeve of the jacket.

Full dress uniform

Full dress is worn with the Royal Stewart kilt and fly plaid, Balmoral headwear with a feather plume, Royal Stewart handknitted hose and black buckle brogue shoes. His jacket is a No 1 dress jacket made in black barathea with a black velvet collar and gold insignia on the right-hand sleeve. With this jacket, the Sovereign's Piper wears a leather cross belt and waist belt and buckle. His fine dress sporran is made of white horsehair with black horsehair tassels. This dress uniform is worn for State Banquets, Garter Day, State Opening of Parliament, Trooping the Colour, diplomatic receptions and evening playing at the Palace of Holyroodhouse.

The piper's working dress is worn for daily playing duties and when carrying out his role as an Honorary Page of Presence for audiences/credentials, garden parties and investitures. This uniform has a patrol jacket in navy barathea with gold insignia on the sleeve and a hand-woven royal insignia badge on the left-hand front pocket and is worn without a plaid or belts (headdress is only worn when playing outside). All tartan kilts are worn as working dress with a diced Balmoral cap, plain-coloured hose and black ghillie brogue shoes. The sporran is made of black patent with a royal crest on the front.

The third outfit (*see* page 170), strictly for use at Balmoral Castle in Scotland, comprises a Balmoral tartan kilt, a Balmoral jacket with coats of arms and black piping on the collar, diamond shaped silver buttons engraved with coats of arms for the jacket and sleeves, silver insignia on the right-hand sleeve, a Balmoral cap, handknitted Balmoral tartan hose, and black buckle brogue shoes. The dress Balmoral jacket, worn when playing each evening at dinner and also for the two Ghillie Balls, has a leather cross belt and leather waist belt and buckle and the uniform includes a full Balmoral tartan piper's plaid and a dress horsehair sporran. For the Balmoral Castle Summer Court and for daily duties at Balmoral Castle, the working dress patrol jacket and corresponding accessories are worn.

Below: Working dress uniform with an Ancient Hunting Stewart tartan kilt and black patent leather sporran. The patrol jacket is in navy barathea with gold insignia on the right hand sleeve and handwoven royal insignia on the left hand front pocket. This uniform is worn without a plaid or belts. The piper pictured is Alistair Cuthbertson who was the Sovereign's Piper from 2006–2008.

Working dress uniform

Balmoral full dress uniform

Above: Derek Potter, the Sovereign's Piper 2008–2012, wearing Balmoral full dress uniform at Balmoral Castle. The uniform comprises a Balmoral tartan kilt and plaid, a horsehair dress sporran, a Balmoral cap, handknitted Balmoral tartan hose and buckle brogue shoes. The Balmoral dress jacket has silver royal insignia on the right hand sleeve and is worn with a leather cross belt and a leather waist belt.

Pipe Major Derek William James Potter RVM, Sovereign's Piper from 2008–2012: Personal Memoir

In June 2008, after having served as Pipe Major with the Royal Scots Dragoon Guards, I was posted to London to carry out the role of "the Sovereign's Piper", a post first held by Angus McKay at the request of Queen Victoria.

On arrival, I then travelled to each of the Royal Palaces and Residences to conduct my primary playing duties each morning and to carry out the duties as an Honorary Page of the Presence.

At each of the formal events I would be in attendance – from State Banquets, Garter Day, the Queen's Birthday Parade, Investitures, Audiences, Credentials, Garden Parties and Receptions – and at each I carried out the various duties.

During my tenure as Sovereign's Piper I was very fortunate to assist in many memorable events: the State Visit of President Obama, the Visit of Pope Benedict XVI, the Royal Wedding of HRH Prince William and Catherine Middleton, the Diamond Jubilee celebrations and the London 2012 Olympics, to name a few.

I was required to travel to the Palace of Holyroodhouse and Balmoral Castle for Summer Court, where I would also play in the evening for various dinner guests.

At Balmoral the Pipe Major stays for the duration of the Summer Court and I had the privilege of playing for Her Majesty and Members of the Royal Family carrying on a long-standing tradition in place since 1843. As the tower clock chimed each morning at 9 o'clock, the sound of pipes would strike in and this would herald the Pipe Major's morning set, playing for fifteen minutes each day, no matter the weather conditions, rain, hail or shine.

My uniforms were made by Kinloch Anderson and were different for each part of the day that I was on duty.

It was a great honour to have been appointed as the thirteenth Sovereign's Piper and to have served in this role personally for Her Majesty Queen Elizabeth II.

Pipe Major Derek Potter has composed six piping tunes which he has dedicated to Kinloch Anderson Scotland. They have been recorded by pipers from the Royal Scots Dragoon Guards Pipe Band: "The Castle Grey of Edinburgh", "The Reel of the Blue Loch", "The Heather of the Glen", "The Dance of the Thistle", "The Life of the Sundial", "The Romance of the Highlands".

For information about these tunes please see the Kinloch Anderson Scotland website: www.kinlochanderson.com

Above: The Massed Pipes and Drums of the Royal Scots Dragoon Guards, appearing at the Edinburgh Military Tattoo, August 2019.

The Royal Scots Dragoon Guards
Written by Brigadier Sir Melville Jameson, KCVO, CBE, CStJ

The Royal Scots Dragoon Guards are Scotland's senior regiment and its only regular cavalry. The regiment was formed in 1971 from the union of two famous regiments, the 3rd Carabiniers and the Royal Scots Greys. The 3rd Carabiniers had themselves been constituted in 1922 from the amalgamation of the old 3rd Dragoon Guards and the Carabiniers (6th Dragoon Guards). The history of the Royal Scots Dragoon Guards therefore is the record of three ancient regiments. Through the Royal Scots Greys they can claim to be the oldest surviving cavalry of the line in the British Army. They form part of the Royal Armoured Corps and, though horses have been replaced by tanks and armoured cars, it is the cavalry spirit of the past which provides the inspiration for the future.

Their Colonel in Chief is Her Majesty The Queen and the Deputy Colonel in Chief is HRH The Duke of Kent.

The predecessors of the regiment have an illustrious history spanning 300 years. They have two main battle honours: Waterloo (1815), when during the famous charge of the Greys, Napoleon's Eagle Standard was captured by Sergeant Ewart (this can be seen in the Regimental Museum in Edinburgh Castle); and the other main battle honour is Nunshigum in Burma during the Second World War, when the 3rd Carabiniers drove the Japanese Army from the Nunshigum Ridge and played a heroic part in halting the Japanese advance into India.

During the Cold War years, post Second World War, the regiments were armoured, mainly based in Germany and equipped with main battle tanks. Since those days, the Royal Scots Dragoon Guards have been deployed across the world seeing active service in Iraq and Afghanistan and peace-keeping with the United Nations in Cyprus.

The regiment is now based at Leuchars in Scotland and has rerolled as a light cavalry regiment specialising in reconnaissance and taking part in training and NATO operations in Eastern Europe and overseas.

The regimental band and the pipes and drums have played such a very important part in the history of the regiment. Musicians have been on the establishment since very early times. The forebears of the regiment would have had trumpets, kettle drums and hautbois (oboes). Mid 19th century came the wonderful mounted bands. The mounted band of the Royal Scots Greys – on grey horses, and black drum horse with kettle drummer and white bearskin – performed at the coronation of King George VI in 1937.

Cavalry regiments do not traditionally have pipes and drums, so it was not until 1946, following the Second World War and mechanisation, that the Pipes and Drums of the Royal Scots Greys were formed. The then Colonel in Chief, King George VI, took a great interest in the band and granted the wearing of the Royal Stewart Tartan.

Following the birth of the Military Band of the Royal Scots Dragoon Guards in 1971, although it was not the custom of military bands and pipes and drums to play together, they made an album called "Farewell to the Greys", on which was the first ever recording of "Amazing Grace" with bagpipes. In 1972, having been picked out by BBC Radio, "Amazing Grace" went on to become a massive hit – number one in the charts for six weeks, selling a million copies in the UK and 11 million worldwide, earning the regiment eight gold discs.

Then, very sadly, in 1995 regimental military bands were disbanded leaving the pipes and drums only, but, despite this, recording success continued with the release of various very successful albums, particularly "Spirit of the Glen – Journey" which won the Classical Brit Award for the Album of the Year in 2009. The Pipes and Drums, who have performed at Grade 1 in the World Pipe Band Championships three times now, go from strength to strength.

The Royal Scots Dragoon Guards, as Scotland's Cavalry, along with its world-famous Pipes and Drums, continue to play a full part in the modern Army of today and remain "Second to None".

Above: The Royal Scots Dragoon Guards, through the Royal Scots Greys, can claim to be the oldest surviving cavalry of the line in the British Army.

Below: The cap badge of the Royal Scots Dragoon Guards features the French Imperial Eagle that was captured by Sergeant Charles Ewart of the Royal Scots Greys from the French 45th Regiment of Foot at the Battle of Waterloo. Behind the eagle are the crossed carbines of the 3rd Carabiniers.

Left: A photograph of HM King George VI that was gifted to WJ Kinloch Anderson in 1952, at the time of the death of His Majesty.

Enclosed was a letter from the Palace, to thank William Anderson & Sons for their service.

BUCKINGHAM PALACE

November 3rd, 1952

Dear Mr. Anderson,

I am now commanded by Queen Elizabeth the Queen Mother to send you the enclosed photograph of The King, which Her Majesty thinks you will like to have in memory of the past few years, when you served His Majesty.

Yours sincerely,

Katharine Seymour

Lady-in-Waiting.

W.J. Kinloch Anderson, Esq.

Right: Prince Henry, The Duke of Gloucester, third son of George V, pictured in his regimental Highland Dress which was made by William Anderson & Sons.

The inscription on the back of this photograph reads: "Presented to WJK Anderson, from Princess Alice, Dowager Duchess of Gloucester. HRH The Duke of Gloucester, Col-in-Chief of the Gordon Highlanders. Regimental outfit was made by Anderson's of George Street in 1938."

Chapter Eight

THE SCOTTISH REGISTER OF TARTANS

THE SCOTTISH REGISTER
OF TARTANS TARTAN

THE Scottish Register of Tartans is the official and definitive database to record, preserve and promote historic and contemporary tartans from Scotland and worldwide. The register is located within the National Archives of Scotland in Edinburgh.

Deirdre Kinloch Anderson, a fifth generation director of the Kinloch Anderson Company, was the leading architect for the establishment of this register. Until 2009, the recording of tartans was carried out by private organisations. The project's aim was to ensure that the recording and codification of tartan was placed in the public domain, safeguarding Scotland's tartan heritage in perpetuity. A commercial operation is always at risk of closure if there is no longer the financial resource for its maintenance. A national register ensures that this iconic part of Scotland's heritage will be supported by government funding.

It took seven years, a Private Member's Bill passed through the Scottish Parliament, including a Parliamentary consultation process and an economic assessment on the value of tartan to Scotland, to fulfil this project.

The Scottish Register of Tartans includes all existing tartan registrations recorded prior to the establishment of this register in 2009 and all new registrations thereafter. Criteria for registration must conform to the Scottish Register of Tartans Act 2008.

The Act deals with many registration issues, including a definition of tartan for registration purposes. The register aims to promote and preserve information about registered tartans, to be a focal point for tartan research and to support the tartan industry in Scotland.

It is fascinating just to browse through the website. Families carrying out

Page 175 and swatch above:
The Scottish Register of Tartans Tartan was designed by Kinloch Anderson to commemorate the establishment of the register in the National Archives of Scotland in February 2009. It was the first tartan to be recorded in the new register. The brown, red and gold colours were inspired by the volumes of the Register of Sasines stored in the Matheson Dome in General Register House.

Opposite: Tartan pattern books archived at Kinloch Anderson in Leith.

Right: Books of tartan swatches from the Kinloch Anderson archive.

genealogical research will find it an invaluable resource in their studies. The website is in the public domain, and detailed images of tartans can be accessed. The tartan reference number, the designer, the registration dates and restrictions are listed, as are the dates of the registration and also the category under which it is registered. The categories are: clan/family, commemorative, corporate, district, fashion, military, name, royal and other.

In the Scottish Parliament

By the time Sir Jamie McGrigor MSP first spoke in the Scottish Parliament in order to submit his Private Member's Bill for an official tartan register, a steering group had been discussing the issue for more than five years.

The group, initiated by Deirdre Kinloch Anderson, included Brian Wilton of the Scottish Tartans Authority, Keith Lumsden of the Scottish Tartans World Register, Robin Blair the Lord Lyon King of Arms, Dr Nick Fiddes of Scotweb, and Alastair Campbell of Airds, Unicorn Pursuivant of Arms. The project's goal was to secure the status of an independent and authoritative tartan register for Scotland and the world. A government-owned register of this national symbol of identity would provide its information freely and be immune from the threat of commercial exploitation.

Many people were surprised to learn that this was not already in existence.

2001

▶ Deirdre Kinloch Anderson initiates discussions regarding a Register of Tartans.

2004

▶ The steering group and Jamie McGrigor MSP (b.1949) discuss the possibility of getting his help to create a Bill to create the Register of Tartans.

2007

▶ Jamie McGrigor introduces the general principles of a Bill to the Scottish Parliament. It is met with a positive response.

Left: Much of the work of the Scottish Parliament is carried out, not in the debating chamber but by cross-party committees. Their discussions are held in rooms such as these.

During the report stage of the Bill, Alastair Campbell of Airds wrote, "The role of Mrs Kinloch Anderson in initiating the whole idea of a Bill has been vital to its successful outcome and this should be given recognition."

During the debate in February 2007, before the Bill's submission, Ken Macintosh MSP, son-in-law of Deirdre and Douglas Kinloch Anderson and future Presiding Officer of the Scottish Parliament, said, "We protect our natural heritage and we are proud of our Highland history, so why do we not protect tartan?" Ken's father was a native Gaelic speaker and a great advocate for the Gaelic language and its continuation into future generations. "My father is the last in a long line of native Gaelic speakers and I am proud that the Parliament has done so much to secure Gaelic – in fact, to save it," he said. "Like my father-in-law who is the fifth in the line of generations of kilt makers in the family, I wonder why we cannot do the same for tartan? Why can we not protect this iconic natural asset?"

It was a very positive debate overall with most MSPs agreeing in principle with Sir Jamie's proposal.

The Bill was submitted in March 2008 and the Economy, Energy and Tourism Committee, convened by Tavish Scott MSP, was appointed as the lead committee in consideration of the Bill.

In October 2008 the Scottish Parliament passed the "Scottish Register of

2008
- In March the Economy, Energy and Tourism Committee is appointed as lead committee in consideration of the Bill.
- In October the Scottish Parliament passes the Bill.
- In November the Bill receives Royal Assent (Pictured right:the Great Seal of Scotland.)

2009
- The web site of the Scottish Register of Tartans is officially launched.

2010
- Deirdre Kinloch Anderson receives an OBE for her services to the textile industry.

Right: Jim Mather MSP, Deirdre Kinloch Anderson and Sir Jamie McGrigor pictured in the Great Hall of Edinburgh Castle at a reception to mark the launch of the Scottish Register of Tartans, November 2008.

Tartans Bill", clearing the way for a national register of tartans in Scotland. There was full cross-party cooperation and consensus on the importance of the Bill and the brand value of tartan for Scotland, with overwhelming positivity about it across the Parliament. Indeed, it was being hailed as an example of cohesion amongst the various political parties.

During the Bill's final round of Parliamentary scrutiny, Sir Jamie – at the time, Conservative MSP for the Highlands and Islands – said, "I have worked with the tartan experts on the options for a Scottish Register of Tartans since 2001, and the road has indeed been a long and winding one. It has also been educational and, on occasion, extremely rocky. Now, at last, we stand on the cusp of achieving the shared and long-held ambition of tartan experts, enthusiasts and the tartan industry, of taking tartan to a new national level for the benefit of all. There has been immense and constant support from representatives of the Scottish tartan industry, particularly from Deirdre Kinloch Anderson of Kinloch Anderson of Leith."

Mr McGrigor also thanked his wife Emma, his mother Mary, his former assistant Joanna Mowat, Blair Urquhart, the late James Scarlett,

The Scottish Government

Jim Mather MSP
Minister for Enterprise, Energy and Tourism

requests the pleasure of the company of

DEIRDRIE KINLOCH-ANDERSON

at a reception to mark the launch of the Scottish Register of Tartans,
in The Great Hall of Edinburgh Castle
on Wednesday, 26ᵗʰ November 2008

6.30 – 8 p.m.
Dress: Tartan   *RSVP details overleaf*

David Cullum, Rodger Evans, Alison Wilson and Mike McElhinney.

Jim Mather, SNP MSP and Minister for Enterprise, Energy and Tourism from 2003 to 2011, said, "Throughout the work on developing a register, I have been genuinely impressed by the joint working among tartan experts and the tartan industry on the way forward."

Gavin Brown, Conservative MSP for Lothian, sat on the Economy, Energy and Tourism Committee in 2008. In the debate during the roundup of the Bill he said, "The two commercial registers that currently exist have done an outstanding job, but a publicly held repository is the safest way to protect our brand and heritage."

On November 13, 2008, the Bill received Royal Assent, and the register's website was officially launched on February 5, 2009. For Deirdre Kinloch Anderson, tartan was finally where it rightfully belonged – in the ownership of the Scottish people.

In order to avoid any confusion with tartan numbers from existing registers, the first tartan to be registered was numbered STR 10,000. It was the Scottish Register of Tartans' own tartan, designed by Kinloch Anderson!

Deirdre was awarded an OBE for her services to the textile industry in January 2010. She wished her father had been alive to have shared this accolade and said, "He used to say to me, 'If you believe you can do it, never take no for an answer.' And, for me, that was the Tartan Register."

Top right: Bruce Crawford, the then Minister for Parliamentary Business, and Sir Jamie McGrigor in November 2008.

Right: Deirdre Kinloch Anderson was awarded an OBE for her services to the textile industry in January 2010.

The Scottish Register of Tartans

This is to certify that the following tartan has met the conditions of registration set out in the Scottish Register of Tartans Act, 2008.

The Scottish Register of Tartans' Tartan

Registration Number: 10,000

Thread count details
K/5 M3 LT6 M3 K23 DT2 K2 DT28 T2 DT28 M2 DT2 M7 N4 M/12
Half sett, full count at pivots

Colour Details
K=BLACK; M=MAROON; LT=LIGHT TAN; DT=DARK TAN;
T=TAN; N=NEUTRAL;

Keeper of the Scottish Register of Tartans
5 February 2009

National Records of Scotland

The Scottish Government

Above: On the back wall of the Kinloch Anderson Heritage Room is a framed certificate of the registration of the Scottish Register of Tartans Tartan, containing a swatch of the woven fabric. It was the first new tartan to be recorded in the register.

Registering a New Tartan

You can register new tartans online at the website www.tartanregister.co.uk. You need to create a user account and then complete and submit an application form. The application form must include a threadcount for your tartan and an electronic image of your design. The application is then processed and checked to see if it meets the criteria for registration before it is added to the register and a fine Certificate of Registration is issued.

The criteria for registration, set out in the Scottish Register of Tartans Act 2008 is as follows:

- New tartans must meet the definition of tartan contained in the Act: a design which is capable of being woven, consisting of two or more alternating coloured stripes which combine vertically and horizontally to form a repeated chequered pattern.
- The design of a new tartan must be unique to the register and not confusingly similar to any other tartan already recorded.

- The name of the tartan must be unique to the register and the applicant must be able to demonstrate their relationship with the proposed name.
- The application fee must accompany the application to register the tartan.

Anyone from anywhere in the world, can register a new tartan – individuals, schools, societies, organisations and corporate groups as well as professional designers and weavers – provided that the tartan meets this criteria for registration.

The Scottish Register of Tartans is administered by the National Records of Scotland, and the Keeper of the Records of Scotland is also the Keeper of the Scottish Register of Tartans. A Scottish Register of Tartans Advisory Group – which is available to give advice and consultation to the Keeper – holds a joint meeting twice annually. Members of the group are taken from representatives of the tartan industry, and include the Lord Lyon.

Tartan Design

While tartan design software can now be readily accessed, and is universally available for recreational use worldwide, Kinloch Anderson has always taken a very specialist approach to all the enquiries they receive in this regard. Tartan cannot be ring-fenced as belonging exclusively to Scottish clans and families, nor does it belong to the Scottish weavers. Tartan is a gift that Scotland has given to the world.

The Scots have spread their wings – they have taken their tartans with them and they have married into other nationalities and cultures. History cannot be re-written with a tartan nor can ancestral roots be changed. What matters is that tartan maintains a link with Scotland, be it through the family or through some other association – perhaps a Scottish location or a Scottish personal contact. Tartan is a symbol of belonging and not a logo of short duration. It lasts a lifetime, indeed, is handed down from one generation to the next and, importantly, it comes with a background story which is officially called a "rationale".

When Kinloch Anderson create a tartan design, time and commitment is given to understand the customer's own ideas for its purpose, its use, its significance and its particular relevance for them. Tartan is a proud and colourful representation of personal identity.

Top: Initial tartan designs are printed digitally but the final chosen design will be woven into fabric.

Middle: Matching yarn colours need to be selected together with an understanding of how these appear when the different coloured threads cross each other.

Bottom: Tartan is a gift that Scotland has given to the world.

Clockwise from the top left: Examples of some Kinloch Anderson corporate design clients – The Merchant Company of Edinburgh, St George's School for Girls, Baxters, Drambuie, Sir Jackie Stewart, The Royal Zoological Society of Scotland (child's kilt worn by Harris Kinloch Anderson), The Caledonian Club.

Clockwise from the top left: Examples of some Kinloch Anderson corporate design clients – Barbour, The City of Edinburgh (Clipper Round the World Yacht Crew 2012), Team Scotland – Commonwealth Games, The Bruntsfield Links Golfing Society, British Caledonian Airways, Scottish Chamber Orchestra, Loretto School.

Above: (Top) Coatee and Vest from the 1920s. (Middle) Kenmore Doublet from the 1920s. (Bottom) Modern Kenmore doublet.

Kinloch Anderson discusses the sett (pattern) and colour preferences with each customer, whilst equal importance is placed on historical background. Initial tartan designs are printed digitally but the final chosen design will subsequently be woven into fabric. Therefore matching yarn colours need to be selected together with an understanding of how these appear when the different coloured threads cross each other. Unlike a flat picture, a woven tartan is three-dimensional. The time taken to design and develop a tartan frequently depends on the number of people involved in the decision making! It is not an instant science. To commission and weave a new tartan design usually takes ten to twelve weeks and then additional time is needed for production of the clothing or other items. The last, but far from least, stage of the design process is its registration in the Scottish Register of Tartans.

The final outcome of a tartan design project may be one single tartan item or a full-scale tartan collection.

Fashion

"From classic to modern" is the title of one of the PowerPoint presentations that Kinloch Anderson shows to new suppliers and customers in order to introduce them to the company. No book about Scottish clothing over a period of 150 years would be complete without referring to fashion.

Clothing and fashion go hand in hand, but whilst you "wear" clothes you "love" fashion – or not, as the case may be! The Kinloch Anderson story has evolved alongside clothing and tartan fashion – whether applied to Highland Dress and kiltwear, menswear, ladieswear or childrenswear.

Kinloch Anderson has the very highest reputation for their expertise in kiltmaking. "The kilt has, through the years, proved itself adaptable to changing fashion and ideas and so has remained a living dress of the day and has not been outmoded or outdated," said Mr WJ Kinloch Anderson in *The Merchant Tailor*, September 1949. The kilt is traditionally worn with a great variety of jacket styles depending on the time of day and the preference of the wearer. The design of two of these is attributed to Kinloch Anderson: the Coatee and Vest and the Kenmore.

Highland Dress has long been popular for younger men, looking for a self-confident image. The 1980s saw a revival in "heritage" and a renewal of cultural awareness in Scotland which allowed for kiltwear to become a demonstration of identity and created the opportunity to cast formality aside.

The "rugged" kilt image associated with sport and Highland games was informally worn with Jacobite shirts, hiking boots and rolled down socks. In the 1990s Kinloch Anderson designed the Breacan, the kilted garment for sporting and informal occasions. The company made 800 Breacans and

"Kinloch"
Jacket

Coatee & Vest

Argyll Jacket

Day Outfit

Gauntlet Style
Kilt Jacket

Day Outfit

Plain Style
Kilt Jacket

Left: The kilt
is traditionally
worn with a
great variety of
jacket styles and
material.

Above: Creating a traditional man's kilt requires knowledge, expertise and painstaking craftsmanship.

(Top to bottom) Cutting, chalking of pleats, the sewing on of the canvas, and completed kilts showing belts and buckles.

kilted skirts in the Commonwealth Games tartan for Scotland's Athletic Team for the Melbourne Games in 1995.

They were voted the best dressed team of the games!

Some contemporary designers have taken the opportunity to "modernise" casual kilts with denim kilts, leather kilts, kilts with pockets, or kilts made out of unconventional materials to impress or to shock. These probably represent a passing phase more than a fundamental change from what most Scots believe to be the finest National Dress in the world. "Long after the trendy modern kilt versions of today have gone out of fashion, the Kinloch Anderson traditional kilt will remain in demand," says Deirdre Kinloch Anderson.

Of course the longterm classic nature of Highland Dress, remaining in fashion as it has, also has implications for the company regarding clothing discounts and shop sales. When the annual sale took place in the George Street shop, the queue on the first day went round the corner to Hanover Street. These sales became counterproductive as a means of stock turnover. The customer knew that the sale garments were neither out of date nor out of fashion – they were simply reduced in price! These sales affected business – people just waited for them.

Tartan has been associated with fashion since the Victorian era when it was particularly popular, worn in royal circles and represented the Establishment. Queen Victoria herself wore dresses made from various tartans which sent out inspiring fashion statements, as does the dress sense of the young royals today – even the royal children! Uniform and costume stretch across the fashion industry. Regiments who served the Queen of The British Empire wore tartan – Scottish regiments wore tartan, Indian regiments wore tartan and indeed all these were serviced by Kinloch Anderson.

The popularity of tartan has grown with different influences. Sir Harry Lauder (1870–1950) the Scottish singer and comedian who toured the world for over 40 years performing in full Highland regalia – kilt, sporran, tam o'shanter and holding the cromach – was, according to Sir Winston Churchill "Scotland's greatest ever ambassador" and "rendered measureless service to the Scottish race". The Bay City Rollers, a Scottish pop band who by early 1975 were the biggest group since The Beatles, were deemed the "tartan teen sensation from Edinburgh" and distinctively wore calf-length tartan trousers and tartan scarves. Vivienne Westwood used tartan designs in her collections, and her flamboyant interpretations caught the imagination of many. Tartan is beloved by the French fashion house of Chanel. For ladies, tartan has skilfully found its way from the arisaid and the tartan sash to every skirt style imaginable: kilted, mini, maxi, box pleated, high waisted, hip waisted, bias cut and so many more.

Left: The Kinloch Anderson
Breacan – a kilted garment
for informal and sporting
occasions. The group
pictured are wearing
Tartan Army tartan kilts.

Kinloch Anderson and fashion have frequently come together, both at home and probably even more so overseas. In the 1980s the Kinloch Anderson tartan and tweed skirts were at the height of fashion and could be found in all the major cities of Europe, as well as in America and the Far East.

In the 21st century the Kinloch Anderson 1868 Collection was designed as a modern menswear range based on Kinloch Anderson's former tailoring heritage. It was launched in 2016 for sales in the shop and online. Its "fashionable" concept remains valid, and the 1868 Kinloch Anderson jackets have been a particular success.

Probably the biggest impact on how fashion is portrayed has come from the media. In the 1860s, fashion was found in magazines – *Harpers Bazaar* was one of the first. Then in the next century, as colour television moved into more and more homes until there is now hardly a dwelling place without one, it put fashion in front of people every day. The impact was huge. Neither should we forget the film industry; such films as *Rob Roy* (1995) *Braveheart* (1995) and more recently *Outlander*, have increased a demand for kilts and Scottish clothing as seen in these films.

Above: A silk dress in
the Buchanan tartan,
showcased on the catwalk
of the Coronation Festival,
held in Buckingham Palace
Gardens, July 2013.

Left: A Kinloch Anderson
1868 jacket.

Clothing fashion begins with the famous fashion houses who produce exciting new clothing designs for the catwalk at their renowned fashion shows. Some of these designs are first and foremost taken up by the buyers of the luxury market for exclusive sale in their finest shops. This fashion status is short lived because the buyers of the multiples will identify some aspect of that fashion – perhaps baggy trousers, long flared skirts, certain colour combinations or simply just an opening in the shoulder sleeves – which they introduce into the mass market. If this is successful, it then destroys the exclusive nature of the "fashion" at the top end of the marketplace. Remarkably, this cycle of events has never brought down tartan. Cheap copied tartans, known in the trade as "tartan tat", thrive worldwide but have never destroyed the demand for tartan to be proudly worn for the most prestigious occasions, weddings, banquets or royal garden parties. There is no fashion brand stronger than tartan.

Right: The Sheriffmuir is a high-collared evening jacket frequently made in velvet. Celtic buttons adorn the garment on the front, on the flaps and also the cuffs and epaulettes. The jacket looks particularly stunning when worn with a seven-button waistcoat.

Kinloch Anderson is still at the forefront of tartan and Highland Dress today.

Chapter Nine

JOHN WILLIAM KINLOCH ANDERSON

SIXTH GENERATION

TO FOLLOW in the footsteps of five generations who have shown remarkable commitment, leadership and also resilience to the difficult circumstances that have confronted them, is no light undertaking. Douglas and Deirdre decided that all their children, Claire, Peter and John, should be made aware that entry into the company could not be taken for granted and that they should first and foremost pursue their own interests and their talents – and so they did! Although the youngest of the three children, it was John William Kinloch in 2000 who first approached his parents with a view to joining the company.

John was educated at the Edinburgh Academy and Merchiston Castle School. He was a natural sportsman and achieved a great deal in several sports. When at Merchiston, he played rugby for Scottish Schools, both at U15 and U18 age group, and then subsequently for both Scottish Students and Scotland U21. John recalls one such Scotland U21 match was notable not just that they beat their English counterparts, which was rare in itself, but that the Scotland and British Lion prop Tom Smith, who was playing that day, managed to miss the bus departing Murrayfield – allegedly having slept in – and met the team somewhere around the Scottish Borders en route to the game!

In his last year at school he was selected for an exchange to the Southport School in Queensland Australia, where he played rugby for the school and then represented Queensland Schools. As an athlete, he was both Scottish Schools and Scotland U20 Triple Jump champion and went on to represent Scotland at that level. As a good tennis player he landed himself a holiday job as a tennis coach at the Pacific Club in Hong Kong which was an enviable summer holiday job through the years whilst at university.

Page 191 and above: The Kinloch Anderson Sundial tartan was designed for the 150th Anniversary of the company. W Joseph Kinloch Anderson donated a sundial to the City of Edinburgh in 1890, and this sundial was restored by Kinloch Anderson in 2018 as part of the 150th Anniversary celebrations. The sandstone colour relates to the sundial, the green to Inverleith Park where it stands, and the blue to the Water of Leith which runs close to the location of the Kinloch Anderson Company in Leith. The three gold lines stand for the company's three Royal Warrants of Appointment as Tailors and Kiltmakers, and the six fine burgundy lines represent six generations of the company's family ownership and management.

Opposite: John Kinloch Anderson.

Right: John playing on
Merchiston Castle School's
Rugby Tour of Japan in 1989.

John took an honours degree in Sports Science and Recreation Management at Loughborough University. He represented the university first team both at 15-a-side and, notably, at 7-a-side where the university made it all the way through to the Twickenham Sevens Tournament. After graduating, he then worked for a number of years in the fitness industry with the prestigious Champneys luxury health spa resorts in the centre of London.

Undoubtedly the qualities associated with sport have been invaluable to John's career in business: commitment, discipline, respect, sportsmanship, teamwork, friendship, courage and loyalty. Initially it was considered important to keep his involvement with the company as open and flexible as possible, to make sure that the business relationship with both his father and his mother worked well, particularly as he had been away from home for several years. So, while he was learning about retailing, tartans and Highland Dress, he took a postgraduate certificate of Management Studies at Napier University. The trial period worked well and provided everyone with the confidence to proceed.

Claire Deirdre Kinloch Anderson

John's elder sister, Claire, was a graduate of Cambridge University and first chose an acting career, and then was a TV film producer and director with the BBC before she married. Claire and her husband, Ken Macintosh, have six children: Douglas, Catriona, Lachie, Annie, Isobel and Ruth. Claire was living in Glasgow

2000
▶ The world celebrates the start of the new millennium
▶ Dr Harold Shipman is found guilty of murdering fifteen of his own patients.
▶ Russian submarine *Kursk* sinks in the Barents Sea, killing all 118 crew.
▶ George W Bush (b.1946) wins the US Presidential election.

2001
▶ Wikipedia is launched.
▶ Foot-and-mouth outbreak in the UK causes a crisis in British agriculture.
▶ 9/11 attacks in the United States prompt President Bush to declare a 'War on Terror'.

2002
▶ Queen Elizabeth II celebrates her Golden Jubilee.
▶ 170 people die as Chechen rebels hold the audience hostage at Nord-Ost theatre in Moscow.
▶ SARS epidemic begins in China's Guangdong Province

with her family when she spent a short time in the Kinloch Anderson Company. Who else but Claire could live in Glasgow with six children, be the tennis coach for her local tennis club, and also cover for the maternity leave of the Kinloch Anderson sales and marketing manager? Then, as her family were growing up, she started her own film production company, KAmac Productions Ltd, and she made the documentary film which tells the story of the restoration of the Kinloch Anderson Sundial in 2018. Her husband Ken was elected Presiding Officer of the Scottish Parliament in 2016.

Peter Douglas Kinloch Anderson

John's elder brother, Peter, went to Shrewsbury School and began his career in the hotel industry, followed by the cruise line industry. He then worked for the Kinloch Anderson Company, living in Shanghai and covering all matters arising from a menswear licence agreement with a Chinese company which lasted for just three years. However, Peter actually reckons that the time of his life most relevant to this book was when he was fourteen years old. The digital electronic chalking machine (DECS) at the Kinloch Anderson Restalrig factory was introduced in order to computerise and chart the pleat settings for the tartan skirts. Peter spent his summer holidays programming skirt patterns for all the tartans in the Kinloch Anderson catalogue, including all the size differences for the American and emerging Japanese markets.

Left: Kinloch Anderson "Family Ensemble", with Claire (flute), Douglas (violin), John (piano), Deirdre (cello) and Peter (cello). Credit: *People* magazine.

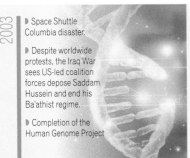

2003
▶ Space Shuttle Columbia disaster.

▶ Despite worldwide protests, the Iraq War sees US-led coalition forces depose Saddam Hussein and end his Ba'athist regime.

▶ Completion of the Human Genome Project

2004
▶ Facebook is created by Mark Zuckerberg (b.1984).

▶ The Olympic Games are held in Athens.

▶ Tsunamis resulting from an earthquake cause mass destruction and a huge death toll in countries around the Indian Ocean.

2005
▶ Death of Pope John Paul II

▶ Prince Charles marries Camilla Parker Bowles

▶ Terrorist bombings in London

▶ Hurricane Katrina causes widespread damage to Florida and the Gulf Coast in the US.

Vision Magazine, Spring 2019:
"Family Tartans", by David Lee.

"With the sixth generation at the helm, Kinloch Anderson is living proof that family firms can survive and thrive if they are willing to adapt and innovate."

An old adage claims that the first generation creates a family business, the second spends the money and the third destroys it. Cynically simplistic perhaps, but statistics suggest only 3 per cent of family businesses make it to the fourth generation and only 1 per cent to the fifth.

By that measure, Kinloch Anderson is a rare phenomenon, with current chief executive John Kinloch Anderson the sixth-generation family leader.

Tartan is at the heart of that story. Scotland's relationship with tartan is complex. As a national symbol, it is often derided as part of the "tartan and shortbread" stereotype, deployed by critics as a sign that modern Scotland has failed to cast off couthy historic emblems.

Yet as John Kinloch Anderson points out, the younger generation embraces tartan, especially the kilt, as much as any before it. "I think tartan is timeless," he says. "It's about belonging, it's about culture, and people still feel strongly

John and his father, working together as two generations of the family, provided the great potential of combining experience and acquired knowledge of the one generation with new ideas and up-to-date understanding of technologies of the other. As John himself said, "We've not got to where we are by doing things the way they've always been done. Each generation has

EVENTS IN THE TIME OF
THE SIXTH GENERATION

2006
▶ The United Nations Human Rights Council is established.

▶ Execution of Saddam Hussein (1937–2006).

▶ North Korea carries out its first nuclear test.

2007
▶ The first iPhone is launched by Apple CEO Steve Jobs (1955–2011).

▶ Disappearance of Madeleine McCann.

▶ Global financial crisis.

2008
▶ Beijing, China hosts the summer Olympics.

▶ Large Hadron Collider is inaugurated at Geneva.

▶ Barack Obama (b.1961) becomes the first African-American President of the USA.

affiliated to it, especially family tartans. It can also be used at the highest level of haute couture by top designers. It is very versatile."

At the other end of the market, John is too diplomatic to utter the phrase "tartan tat", often used to describe the plethora of shops, especially in central Edinburgh, selling tartan – and shortbread, whisky and the rest – to a burgeoning tourist market demanding "Scottish souvenirs".

He has no issue with such shops selling tartan products, often imported, at low prices. "We know what we are trying to achieve and concentrate on, rather than worry what others are doing."

Indeed, cut-price sales of tartan kilts and scarves to a mass market could be seen as industry disruption in much the same way as when Kinloch Anderson started selling ready-to-wear men's clothing – incurring the disdain of Edinburgh's master tailors in the 1920s and 30s.

Asked how his firm stands out in this ever-changing, highly competitive market, John says, "Real provenance and an expectation of high-quality products and service. What we do has not changed radically in 150 years; it's the method of delivery that has changed. Lots of people still come in and enjoy a high level of expertise but we

need to reflect that quality experience online to global customers."

John's increasing focus on digital opportunities reflects how every Kinloch Anderson generation has freshened up the business, from ready-to-wear clothes and ladies' fashion, to exports and brand partnerships. He thinks this is a sign of the greater opportunity to flex a family business: "You definitely have the ability to about-turn and go in a different direction if that is right for the family. You can pass down skills and knowledge through the generations and plan for the long-term as you are not having to deliver short-term returns for investors or shareholders."

John sees the strength of family businesses as "a commitment to the business and willingness to invest time and money", but concedes this can also be a challenge: "The commitment can be very demanding and the nature of a family business will not suit everyone."

John decided he was able to work with his parents, but insists it wasn't based on sentiment. "We are different and have differences of opinion," he admits, "but it's about how you deal with them. The experience of working with my parents has been, and continues to be, invaluable to me."

made a significant change, or moved in a direction to fit with the needs of the time."

Business travel has become faster and easier than ever before, but this means that an SME company (small and medium-sized enterprise) now faces ever-increasing competition. John clearly decided to continue the policy for

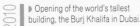

2009
▶ Swine flu global pandemic.
▶ The Parliamentary expenses scandal causes widespread anger amongst the British public.

2010
▶ Opening of the world's tallest building, the Burj Khalifa in Dubai.
▶ Volcanic ash from Mount Eyjafjallajökull, erupting in Iceland, causes widespread disruption to European travel.

2011
▶ A study by BOP Consulting attempts to understand the impact of Edinburgh's Festivals in cultural, social and environmental terms. Of tourists questioned, 33% said their sole reason for coming to Scotland was the Edinburgh Festivals. (The study was updated in July 2016.)

the company to be "the best of British style and fashion with a strong Scottish emphasis", and to maintain its position at the top end of a niche market in Scottish clothing and textiles. It has also been a definite decision to maintain the diversity of the company and to avoid "putting all our eggs into one basket". The result of this policy is that, as the fluctuating market situation changes, one sector of the company can be supported by others and the longevity of the company is thereby maintained.

In John's generation, businesses have had to adapt fast to changing technological advances. Whilst being a traditional business in a number of ways, the company still needs to adapt, as it has always done, in order to thrive and succeed. The twenty-first century has seen the introduction to the company of a number of technology-related activities: e-commerce which continually evolves and contributes to the business each year, IT systems upon which businesses progressively depend, and, most recently, a company-wide ERP system (enterprise resource planning) to integrate all the various functions of the company. The ERP system provides more informative and immediate data, together with an omnichannel selling experience for the customer.

Above: John and his father on the production floor at Leith, wearing their multi-tartan waistcoats given to them as birthday presents by the staff.

Right: Kinloch Anderson taxis in the company's car park in Leith. In 2020 there were ten Kinloch Anderson taxis circulating in the City of Edinburgh, promoting the Kinloch Anderson name and with Kinloch Anderson pictures on the backs of the seats inside.

The Kinloch Anderson Whisky Story

An interesting new venture in the Kinloch Anderson story has been the introduction of the Kinloch Anderson Whisky Collection.

John was primarily involved in all aspects of the design, development and marketing associated with this project.

Kinloch Anderson brings the character of Scotland into its clothing ranges and the taste of Scotland into its whisky. Scotland is renowned for kilts and tartans, whisky and beer, salmon and fishing, castles and stately mansions, and is famous as the home of golf – and all against a background of hills, moors and lochs. The Kinloch Anderson brand fits comfortably with whisky, one of these most famous icons. For centuries the kilt has been worn to fend off the cold, and whisky has been distilled to warm the heart.

The exclusive Kinloch Anderson Whisky Collection, personally selected by the Kinloch Anderson family, features the celebrated Kinloch Anderson tartans on the labelling and the packaging. There are two unique blends – long aged in oak casks – and a well-matured Highland single malt. In addition to these, is a finest 25-year-old malt and grain whisky and a rare 30-year-old single malt.

The Kinloch Anderson Whisky Collection is endorsed by the world's most renowned Scotch whisky expert, Charles MacLean, who reviewed and penned his personal tasting notes for each of the whiskies.

Above: The tasting notes of Kinloch Anderson whisky have been written by renowned whisky expert Charles MacLean.

Below: The Kinloch Anderson Highland Single Malt Scotch Whisky.

Reflections from John Kinloch Anderson

A couple of memories that stand out for John both relate to naturally occurring phenomena. They show just how unpredictable business can be even with the best laid plans.

"In April 2010, I went on a trip to visit some international partners in a variety of countries in Asia. I was there with my father, Douglas, and the plan was that I would return a day or so earlier. So I set off for home and arrived in Amsterdam at the very same time that a volcano in Iceland erupted, creating such a huge ash cloud that it covered large areas of Northern Europe. About twenty countries were closing their airspace to commercial jet traffic. This caused severe flight disruption, so I was stuck in Amsterdam airport with all my luggage in storage under the airport. The result was that Douglas unbelievably arrived home ahead of me and in good shape whilst I reached home days later and distinctly dishevelled!

Above: In 2010, the eruption of the Icelandic volcano Eyjafjallajökull caused travel disruption all over the world.

Above: Flooded buildings in New York City. Hurricane Sandy in 2012 caused damage and disruption across America.

"In 2012, Brooks Brothers, USA approached Kinloch Anderson with a view to having our Highland Dress collection in their famous New York store in Madison Avenue. This was a turn back in time as my grandfather WJ Kinloch Anderson was there in that very store with a very similar partnership concept fifty years previously. I went to New York for the big launch in late October that year. However, at that time, Hurricane Sandy swept in, which turned out to be one of the costliest storms ever to hit the United States, and I recall the hotel was without any power, light or food. Nothing was to be found in any street lower than 40th Avenue where I was based, and this continued for about a week. Brooks Brothers was closed, as were many other stores and the airports. A successful launch was rescheduled the next year."

EVENTS IN THE TIME OF
THE SIXTH GENERATION

2014

▶ The return of the trams to Edinburgh. The project, estimated in 2003 at £375 million, has cost £771 million.

▶ A referendum on Scottish independence is held on September 18. The "No" side wins with 55% compared to 45% for "Yes".

▶ Nicola Sturgeon (b.1970) becomes First Minister of Scotland.

2015

▶ 16- and 17-year-olds get the right to vote in Scottish elections.

▶ The Borders Railway – the longest new domestic railway to be built in the UK for over 100 years – is opened by HM The Queen.

2016

▶ UK electorate votes in favour of leaving the European Union.

▶ Theresa May (b.1956) becomes UK Prime Minister.

▶ Donald Trump (b.1946) wins the US presidential election with 304 seats, with 227 going to Hillary Clinton (b.1947). Clinton wins the public vote.

New Challenges

In 2010 John was made CEO of Kinloch Anderson. He had taken care to gain comprehensive knowledge and experience of all the divisions of the company and establish the respect of the staff. He made new appointments, thereby building his new team of management.

The importance of the support of the wife of the leader of the family business cannot be underestimated. John's wife, Jo, says, "My father ran his own family business and I never wanted to marry into one!" Having done so, her good sense prevailed, and she has a part-time position, principally responsible for the website and digital media, much of which can also be done at home. She turns her hand to anything as required. She has found the company to be much more interesting than she thought. However, she continues to maintain that her family will always be her first priority. John and Jo have two children, Ameline and Harris.

"Longevity has clearly helped Kinloch Anderson," John says. "People want heritage and authenticity, and the longer you go on, the more interesting and relevant your history becomes.

"As I look back on the generations who built this business, I feel proud of what they have achieved, and I am determined to carry things forward to the best of my ability.

"William Anderson, who began it all, saw such changes in the industry: mechanisation, the evolution from bespoke tailoring to mass-produced clothing and the beginnings of military tailoring. Military tailoring became such a feature of the business – from the rise of the Volunteers, through the Boer Wars and Indian campaigns, the First World War, the conflicts of the years before and during the Second World War, and indeed subsequent conflicts which involve our military regiments to the present day."

Thankfully there have been many more years of peace than war, and, for Kinloch Anderson, Highland Dress tailoring remains the "jewel in the crown".

Kinloch Anderson Family Achievements Outwith the Company

The chapters of this book have traced the generations of family leadership in the Kinloch Anderson Company, but other members of the Kinloch Anderson family have made outstanding contributions to our nation and represent additional personal inspiration worthy to be included in this story.

2017
▶ The Queensferry Crossing opens. Queensferry Bridge tartan designed by Kinloch Anderson.

▶ Cyclist Mark Beaumont sets the world record for cycling around the globe.

2018
▶ The V&A Dundee, a design museum, opens to the public.

▶ Scotland co-hosts the European Championships in Glasgow.

2019
▶ Boris Johnson (b.1964) becomes UK Prime Minister.

▶ Amazon forest wildfires declared an international emergency.

▶ The US House of Representatives impeaches Donald Trump. The Senate acquits him.

2020
▶ Devastating Australian bushfires kill an estimated 500 million animals.

▶ The Covid-19 pandemic sweeps the world.

Ronald Kinloch Anderson (1911–1984)

Ronald Kinloch Anderson was Douglas's father's brother and, therefore, John's great uncle. He was born in Edinburgh in 1911 to William Kinloch Anderson (1874–1949) and Mary Wilson, a younger brother for Elsa and Kinloch.

He studied music at the University of Edinburgh and continued his training at the Royal Conservatory of Music, with Malcolm Sargent conducting and Herbert Howells teaching composition. In 1933 he studied piano in Berlin and thereafter studied harpsichord in Fontainebleau, France.

The Scotsman, **October 31, 1936 carried the following article:**

PIANO RECITAL

"Mr Ronald Kinloch Anderson, a young Edinburgh pianist, who is a musical graduate of the University, and was awarded a Caird Scholarship four years ago, gave a recital in the Freemasons' Hall last night, which revealed him as already an artist of remarkable attainments. His programme included Bach's English Suite in A major, Schumann's Sonata in G minor, Op. 22; Beethoven's Thirty-Two Variations in C minor, Mozart's Sonata in F major (K.332), and Chopin's Fantasie in F minor, Op.49. It was a programme of a nature to test a pianist at every point. Mr Anderson has a brilliant technique and his clean-cut rendering of the Bach Suite, was admirable alike in understanding and execution... Mr Anderson's recital impressed the hearer, also with a sense

Right: Ronald Kinloch Anderson.

of something individual. He has youth on his side. Art comes to its full growth only with maturity, and with the good fortune which everyone who heard his recital will wish him, Mr Anderson may go far.

In 1939, Robert Masters, Nannie Jamieson, Muriel Taylor and Ronald Kinloch Anderson met to form a piano quartet. Besides all their concerts at home, they made three world tours and became internationally known as the Robert Masters Quartet.

Left: The Robert Masters Quartet at Broadcast House, Sydney, in 1950. Left to right, Robert Masters, Nannie Jamieson, Ronald Kinloch Anderson and Muriel Taylor.

During the Second World War, Ronald served in Royal Air Force (RAF) Intelligence where his perfect command of the German language was invaluable. When Yehudi Menuhin formed the Bath Festival Orchestra (later known as the Menuhin Festival Orchestra) he used players he had worked with in London recording sessions including Ronald Kinloch Anderson. From 1957–1963 Ronald was the harpsichordist of the Bath Festival Orchestra with which he gave a concert in the Royal Festival Hall in 1958.

In 1963 he became Artistic Director at EMI Records and collaborated with great artists such as, Svetlanov, Rostropovich, Barbirolli, Richter, Victoria Delos Angeles, Maria Montserrat Caballé, Adrian Bolt, Janet Baker and, of course, Yehudi Menuhin. Ronald was known for his warmth, his sensitive musicianship and for his great skill in bridging the gap between live performance and studio recording.

Douglas Kinloch Anderson clearly remembers Uncle Ronald's visit to him at the George Street shop when he was accompanied by a rather dapper man wearing a black fedora hat and long black cloak. Following warm greetings, he introduced Douglas to his friend, Sir John Barbirolli.

Ronald loved fine dining and took Douglas and Deirdre to dinner in a fashionable restaurant in Chelsea, London on the night of their engagement.

Ronald Kinloch Anderson died in London on January 22, 1984 having fulfilled the prophecy of that 1936 Scotsman critic: "Mr Anderson may go far".

He requested his funeral to be a concert given by famous musicians!

Sir William Eric Kinloch Anderson KT FRSE (1936–2020)

Eric Kinloch Anderson was Douglas's brother and John's uncle. When still at school at George Watson's College, Edinburgh and asked by a teacher what he wanted to do, he replied, "It would be quite fun to be headmaster." He said, "I thought I would go into the family business until my brother declared his intention to do that."

He became very interested in English literature and wanted to share his enthusiasm with other people. Following his degrees from St Andrews and Oxford Universities, he chose a career in teaching and went to the very top of his profession.

At the beginning of his career at Gordonstoun School, near Elgin, he taught and was mentor to Prince Charles. As Housemaster of Arniston House, Fettes College, Edinburgh, Tony Blair was amongst his pupils. When Blair became Prime Minister, he named Eric as one of the most influential people in his life. Eric went on to become Headmaster of Abingdon School, Oxford, then Shrewsbury School, Shropshire, followed by Eton College in 1980, a position he held for fourteen years. There he taught two more future prime ministers, David Cameron and Boris Johnson. His appointment as Rector of Lincoln College, Oxford followed before he returned to be Provost of Eton.

When he died, Simon Henderson, Eton's Headmaster said, "Sir Eric's contribution to Eton was unparalleled in modern times. He was one of the school's greatest ever Headmasters and then one of our finest Provosts. He was a wonderful schoolmaster, a fine scholar and an inspiring and visionary man – but above all a kind, loyal, humble and an utterly authentic man."

In his later life, he used his knowledge and intellectual talents on a great

Below: Abbotsford House, the family home of Sir Walter Scott.

many Trusts and Charitable Boards. These included his chairmanship of The National Heritage Lottery fund and his position as a Trustee of the £12 million, two-year refurbishment project of Abbotsford House, the family home of Sir Walter Scott. He was awarded Honorary Degrees by five different universities, was a Fellow of the Royal Society of Edinburgh and an Honorary Member of The Merchant Company of Edinburgh. He was appointed Knight of the Thistle in 2002.

Yet what motivated him most was to instil in young people a love of learning and great literature, and to have a positive influence on their lives. There is a very long list of pupils who received his encouragement and support who subsequently became famous but, for Eric, every pupil was equally important. He was a remarkable man.

Left: Sir Eric Kinloch Anderson (in 1997) with former Prime Minister Tony Blair, who named him as one of the most influential people in his life.

Left: Eton College, where Eric was Headmaster for fourteen years.

David Kinloch Anderson, Lord Anderson of Ipswich KBE, QC (b. 1961)

David is family member who has indisputably made an outstanding contribution to our country. He is Eric's son and John's cousin. As a schoolboy, he was awarded a scholarship to Eton College, and the family teased his father that this assisted his appointment as Headmaster of Eton thereafter!

David made his career in the legal profession as a barrister. He is quoted as being "clever, urbane and economical in his approach", and with "impeccable discernment and judgement" (Chambers & Partners, 2019). He was described as the UK's "Legal Personality of the Year" in 2015.

David acquired legal knowledge of the European Union, human rights, public and constitutional law, developed with the help of skills learned working in Washington DC and Brussels, and teaching at King's College London. He has appeared frequently in Strasbourg (European Court of Human Rights) and Luxembourg (EU courts), as well as in the full range of English courts and tribunals. He has written extensively on EU law and has a long-standing association with the Centre of European Law at King's College London.

As the UK's Independent Reviewer of Terrorism Legislation (2011–2017), David developed a reputation as a national and international authority on national security law and practice. His reports on counterterrorism, counter-extremism and surveillance law have been widely cited in

Above: David Kinloch Anderson, Lord Anderson of Ipswich, pictured in his Parliamentary robes.

Parliament and in the highest British and European courts; two became blueprints for the Investigatory Powers Act 2016. He has also served as a Council of Europe Human Rights Monitor and a Recorder of the Crown Court. He continues to sit as a Judge of the Courts of Appeal of Jersey and Guernsey.

In July 2018 David was introduced to the House of Lords as a crossbench peer, where he is active in a number of fields and serves on the EU Justice Committee.

In the Queen's Birthday Honours in 2018 he was appointed a Knight of the British Empire for services to National Security and Civil Liberties.

David has outstanding intellectual ability, readily combined with common sense and thoughtful humanity – and he keenly acknowledges his Scottish roots. Deirdre Kinloch Anderson is honoured that David has written the foreword to her book.

Lieutenant Eric MacLeod Milroy (1887–1916)

Eric Milroy was John's great, great uncle who, as has been mentioned earlier in this book, at the age of 29, tragically lost his life in the First World War – as did other members of the family. He is particularly admired by John for his great achievements in the game of rugby. Like Eric Milroy, John was a keen rugby player and remains a rugby enthusiast.

Eric Milroy played for Scotland in almost every international match from 1911–1914 and toured with the British team to South Africa in 1910. On January 1, 1913 he played for Scotland in the international against France at Parc de Princes. He and French player Marcel Burgun – who would also be lost in the war – took to the field for what would be the last international match between the two countries before the outbreak of the First World War. Eric captained Scotland in his twelfth and final international match against England on March 21, 1914.

Eric's family still cherish a poignant letter that he wrote to his mother in pencil on military paper the day before he died in the Battle of the Somme in July 1916. "We are in some slight trouble tomorrow so I am just warning you that there is to be no 'keeping well back'. (His mother always used to say to him before a rugby match, "Now keep well back, Eric" – not easy advice for a scrum half!)

Above: Eric Milroy.

Below: Scotland XV v France, 1 January 1 1913, Parc des Princes.

Above: Lachlan Ross and Romain Cabanis, 11-year-old descendants of Eric Milroy and Marcel Burgun respectively, with the Auld Alliance Trophy at Murrayfield Stadium in 2018.

Above: The Eric Milroy trophy for kicking.

In the aftermath of his early death, his mother presented the Eric Milroy Trophy for kicking, to George Watson's College. This trophy continues to be awarded to this day and indeed was won by John's father in 1956. Other winners have included the Scottish Rugby International players, Gavin Hastings and Scott Hastings.

In 2017, a veterans' rugby tournament was organised to be played in the areas where over half a million French and Allied soldiers were killed or wounded. This was also intended to highlight the price that was paid by so many young rugby players from both countries. The tournament was called "Challenge Eric Milroy".

This veterans' rugby tournament inspired the idea of having an Auld Alliance Trophy awarded to the winners of the Scotland v France International match each year. The names of Eric Milroy and Marcel Burgun, each of whom captained their national teams and who played against each other in 1913, are inscribed on the trophy. Both players were killed in the First World War.

This trophy also represents the ultimate sacrifice made by rugby players of both nations, and embodies the Auld Alliance that was renewed in the Great War.

It was first presented to the winners of the Six Nations match between Scotland and France on February 11, 2018 and was carried onto the pitch at Murrayfield, Edinburgh by Lachlan Ross and Romain Cabanis, 11-year-old descendants of Milroy and Burgun.

Unsung Heroes
Of course, apart from those who have received public recognition for their achievements, there are many unsung heroes in the wider Kinloch Anderson family.

There are those with noteworthy achievements in the arts, education, sport, commerce, farming, politics, religion and community life. We are deeply grateful to them all.

The 150th Anniversary of Kinloch Anderson

150th Anniversary Sundial Restoration and Garden Party

On Saturday June 16, 2018, Kinloch Anderson celebrated the 150th Anniversary of the founding of the company with a garden party in the Sundial Garden of Inverleith Park, Edinburgh.

Earlier in that year, Kinloch Anderson had been approached by the Friends of Inverleith Park regarding the restoration of the sundial that had been gifted to the city of Edinburgh in 1890 by William Joseph Kinloch Anderson. (His life and times have been recalled in Chapter Two of this book.)

Below left: *The Scotsman* newspaper article published on Saturday June 16, the day of the 150th Anniversary Garden Party in Inverleith Park.

THE SCOTSMAN
ON SATURDAY

THE SCOTSMAN Saturday 16 June 2018   SCOTSMAN.COM @THESCOTSMAN

Kilt firm marks anniversary with sundial refurb and special tartan

By **EMMA NEWLANDS**

An Edinburgh-based kilt specialist is marking its 150th anniversary today with the unveiling of the refurbished version of a sundial it gifted to the city in 1890.

The Kinloch Anderson Sundial was donated by Councillor W. Joseph Kinloch Anderson, a second-generation leader of the firm, and has been the centrepiece of Inverleith Park's Sundial Garden since it opened in 1891.

The kilt firm is behind the refurbishment after being approached by Friends of Inverleith Park, and felt it would be an excellent way to celebrate its anniversary this year, having originally started out as a tailoring business.

The project includes adding surrounding cobblestones, and information boards giving details about the history and heritage of the item.

"We're very proud and pleased with what we're doing," senior director Deirdre Kinloch Anderson told The Scotsman.

"I would like this to be a historic monument. I would like it to be a credit to Kinloch Anderson and a credit to the city of Edinburgh and I would hope that it will be admired and appreciated by as many people as possible. It's going to look fantastic," added Kinloch Anderson, whose husband Douglas is the firm's chairman and her son John, the sixth-generation chief executive.

The firm has also created a special sundial tartan to mark the occasion, based on the Anderson Clan tartan in a nod to the firm's founder William Anderson, and including three gold lines to represent each of its Royal Warrants as tailors and kiltmakers to The Queen, The Duke of Edinburgh and The Prince of Wales. The tartan will be used to cover the sundial before its unveiling and decorates a range of products including ties and notebooks.

The festivities will be marked by a celebration attended by family, friends and business colleagues, and former Queen's piper Derek Potter will welcome guests and escort the Lord Provost.

Lord Provost Councillor Frank Ross said: "I am delighted to see the historic sundial restored as a striking focal point in this garden. Thank you to Kinloch Anderson for both gifting and, 127 years later, reviving this centrepiece, a fitting celebration of their 150th anniversary."

John Kinloch Anderson said recently that the firm aims to fuse digital opportunities with traditional values of service and quality of product.

emma.newlands@jpress.co.uk

↑ Senior director Deirdre Kinloch Anderson pictured with the special sundial tartan created in honour of the project and anniversary

↑ The sundial was donated by Councillor W. Joseph Kinloch Anderson, a second-generation leader of the firm, in 1890

Above: The Sundial Tartan Collection of products featured tartan-covered notebooks each inserted with an informative leaflet. A mini tartan notebook was given as a souvenir to all the guests who came to the garden party.

Below: Two informative storyboards were placed in the Sundial Garden and tell the story of the sundial, twice gifted to the City of Edinburgh.

The result of this approach was that it stimulated the idea for Kinloch Anderson to restore the sundial and return the restored sundial to the City of Edinburgh in commemoration of the 150th Anniversary of the company. The project received the support and goodwill of both the City of Edinburgh and the Friends of Inverleith.

The sundial had originally been on display at the 1890 International Exhibition of Electricity, Engineering, General Inventions and Industry held at Meggetland in Edinburgh. It was bought by William Joseph when this exhibition ended and was transferred to Inverleith Park with its official opening in May 1891 with due ceremony by Lord Provost Boyd. It has been standing in the park's Sundial Garden ever since.

This gift was reported in *The Scotsman* newspaper, Wednesday, September 10, 1890.

A letter from Mr. Kinloch Anderson to Mr. J.C. Dunlop, Ranger of Inverleith Park, was read, in which Mr Kinloch Anderson intimated the presentation by him of a Sundial to Inverleith Park, 'as an expression of goodwill from the Sunny south to the North Side of the City'. (Applause)

The Lord Provost said they were much indebted to Mr Kinloch Anderson for his gift. He wished he could have sent a little sunshine along with it. Mr. J.C. Dunlop said that they were still open on the North Side to further contributions. (Laughter)

The Restoration of the Sundial

The restoration process for the sundial, required a great deal of time and highly skilled craftsmanship. As well as restoring the stonework, the marble faces, the gnomons and also replacing the top feature, surrounding cobblestones were laid and protective railings replaced.

In bright sunshine, the gnomon casts a shadow which shows the time on the face of the sundial. Sundials provide solar time. Clock time is different, and it can be confusing to check a sundial and clock together. The times on a sundial and clock can be half an hour or more different even though both are correct. Furthermore, we change the clocks one hour ahead of GMT in British Summer Time whilst the position of the sun in the sky does not change.

Two informative storyboards were erected telling the story of the history of the sundial.

Above: The base stones of the sundial prior to restoration.

Middle: Great care was taken to strengthen and protect the top part of the sundial prior to it being uplifted onto a lorry and taken for restoration.

Right: The sundial in the workshop waiting for restoration.

Below: Flatbed truck bringing the restored sundial back to its site in the park.

Right: Graciela Ainsworth (crouching right) masterminding the lowering into position of the restored sundial. Graciela Ainsworth, Sculpture, Conservation, Restoration and Commissions restored the sundial to its former glory.

Right: Former Sovereign's Piper, Derek Potter, leading the Stockbridge Pipe Band, flanked by grandchildren and schoolchildren.

The Garden Party

Despite the inclement weather, the garden party celebration was a happy and gregarious occasion for friends, family, business colleagues and local school-children. Kilts and tartan wear were abundantly in evidence.

Former Sovereign's Piper Derek Potter, welcomed the guests and escorted the Lord Provost Frank Ross on his arrival. Entertainment was provided by the Stockbridge Pipe Band and by the Scottish singer Moira Kerr.

Right: The Lord Provost, Frank Ross, taking time to chat with the children.

Above: If you hold a garden party in Scotland you have to accept the unpredictability of the weather – even if it's in June.

Right: The task was given to the Kinloch Anderson grandchildren to lift the tartan canopy off the sundial– and the driving rain didn't help!

Below: The garden party was an occasion for friends, family, business colleagues and local school children.

Right: (Left to right) Douglas Kinloch Anderson, the Lord Provost Frank Ross, Deirdre Kinloch Anderson, John Kinloch Anderson.

Below: (Clockwise, from top left) Ron Grosset and Liz Small, co-owners of Waverley Books, enjoying a chat with Kinloch Anderson cousin, Jean Ross. John with Sir Andrew Cubie and his wife Heather. Andrew was a non-executive director of the company for 20 years. Claire Kinloch Anderson and Lizzy Hearne. Claire made a video film which tells the story of the sundialm and Lizzy was the garden party's professional photographer. John Duffy and his wife Shirley. John Duffy started working with the company in 1976. Nancy, Bud and Karen McLean came all the way from British Columbia, Canada to join the party.

Above: John Kinloch Anderson giving his welcoming speech.

Right: The Lord Provost of Edinburgh, Frank Ross, cutting the commemorative cake.

Above: Deirdre Kinloch Anderson receiving a thank-you bouquet of sunflowers.

Below: A special 150th Anniversary Luncheon held the following day, Sunday June 17, 2018, at Dalhousie Castle, Midlothian.

Right: The restored sundial, surrounded by newly designed cobblestones and railings, proudly tells the time by the sun in the Sundial Garden of Inverleith Park.

Epilogue

DEIRDRE'S POSTSCRIPT AND CHILDHOOD MEMORIES

KINLOCH ANDERSON
ROMANCE TARTAN

WHEN I went over to greet a visiting group who came to our shop in 2020, their tour guide said, "This is Deirdre Kinloch Anderson, the matriarch of the company." It was intended to be flattering and I took it as such, but, for me, the word matriarch has connotations as the head of the family in a domestic sense rather than as a career woman. I think I have been fortunate to have had a foot in both camps.

I was born in London in 1938, shortly before the outbreak of the Second World War. I only remember the most dreadful noise of the sirens. They created fear and we had to hide. My mother, brother and I moved out of London to Greta Bridge in Yorkshire for about a year. My father joined the Home Guard and stayed in London. His accountancy office in the City of London, close to St Paul's Cathedral, was completely destroyed in the blitz.

My childhood days were spent in the Surrey countryside. My mother was frugal, she never threw away any edible food, we had dripping on toast (which I loved), she saved paper and string, and we found the blackout curtains long after the war was over. There was rationing and in order to have eggs we kept chickens at the bottom of the garden – I used to feed them.

I was always an early riser, and every morning took our large Airedale dog for his walk. I then walked with the girl next door for a mile and a half, with several busy roads to cross, to primary school in Dorking. I was fond of pretty clothes and remember my first *broderie anglaise* party dress. We bought clothes to last in those days.

My idea of beauty was to be natural, and I said that I would never get my hair permed, put on lipstick or wear high heels. My childhood passion was riding. I was going to be the first mounted policewoman and control the Epsom Downs!

At the age of twelve, I went to the girls' boarding school of Malvern Girls' College. The regime and moral values were Victorian, structured, disciplined

Page 217 and swatch above: Romanticism in Scotland of the 18th and 19th centuries was an artistic, literary, musical and intellectual movement. The soft colours of pink, green, blue and purple of the Kinloch Anderson Romance tartan produce an unusually gentle image.

Opposite: On their way from California to Panama in May 2012, the Round the World Yacht Race crews were given a Scottish–American quiz, part of which was to design a sporran (for the New York Tartan Day Parade) and a shield (for the Chieftain of the Scottish Clans). I was asked to judge the entries.

Above: Age 10 with my best pal "Woofy".

and strict. Out-of-school leisure activities were compulsory, as was sport, and most girls played some kind of musical instrument for which daily prep periods were allocated.

My schooldays were happy. I enjoyed being part of a team, was keen to achieve and, if possible, to lead. I remain grateful for the training I received at school. It was focussed on academic excellence and Christian principles, together with music and competitive sport. The school motto was "Vincit qui se vincit" which was translated as "She conquers who conquers herself". It has since been changed to "I can do it" which is more or less the same message but in less belligerent terms.

The art of public speaking was *de rigeur* – we were going to be speaking from the platform, not receiving the flowers! After school my interests broadened into languages and I spent a year at Grenoble University in France. I added Spanish at St Andrews University where I also enjoyed Moral Philosophy, and Logic and Metaphysics, both of which taught me the process of independent thinking.

Books gave me a love of learning which I have done my best to instil into our children, to whom I always read a bedtime story. It provided me with the opportunity to enjoy some of the loveliest children's classics even more than when I was a child. They were allowed to read as long as they wanted and would fall asleep with their book on the bed beside them.

Any career plans I may have entertained never got off the ground, as I married one year after graduation. I had reluctantly obliged my parents by taking a secretarial course. A regrettable legacy of the war was that it left war widows, often with small children to keep, so I was told that secretarial qualifications, together with my degree, would mean that I could always find gainful employment if necessary.

For various reasons, I never seriously thought about employment when our family were young and have no regrets on that score. Much later, in 1990 when the children had grown up, the company moved to Leith and an opportunity came my way to contribute to Kinloch Anderson. I had the enthusiasm of someone half my age. We all seem to remember the times when we were "unlucky", but life is all about recognising a piece of good luck when it comes your way.

Every generation of our company has taken the time to learn from others and to understand how a family company works to best advantage. This is what I set out to do, and some of the next thirty years were the best of my life.

One of the roles that I have most enjoyed has been responding to film crews and journalists, from home and particularly from overseas, looking to feature tartan, kiltmaking and Scotland's National Dress – and of course the Royal

Warrants of Appointment too! Sometimes it would involve famous people – Rory Bremner was a really nice man and so, too, was the chef James Martin. One time a South Korean film crew spent a whole week with us for their global series on companies "Over 100 Years"; they even arrived unannounced at 7 am to film our kiltmakers having their early morning cup of tea and, when privileged with home hospitality, managed to catch me taking our supper out of the microwave!

I have given many talks and speeches on topics such as "what tartan means to Scotland", running a family business, or women in business, but my favourite is giving hands-on demonstrations about tartan and kiltmaking, particularly to schoolchildren.

My position has also taken me to a great many conferences and meetings elsewhere, including a UK Chambers of Commerce Breakfast Meeting held by David Cameron at No 10 Downing Street. I was asked to represent the Scottish Chambers of Commerce at this invitation meeting held to discuss Britain's international trading relationships and how best the government could support SMEs with their global trade.

Perhaps "Married into the family business – thirty years with Kinloch Anderson Ltd" could be the title for another book?

A Scottish Tradition was my first book. I found our company's archive material to be totally absorbing. However, it seemed to be scattered everywhere and so I wanted to make sure that the best of it was kept together and put into a permanent coffee-table book.

Tailored for Scotland is a memoir which covers the evolution of the company, together with lifestyle stories and anecdotes from the six

Top left: Giving a talk on tartan and kiltmaking to the Primary 7 class at Loretto School, Musselburgh, Edinburgh, January 2020.

Top right: Giving a presentation on tartan and kiltmaking in the Wako department store in the Ginza region of Tokyo. This took place during an exhibition held on the Wako exhibition floor to celebrate the Kinloch Anderson Company's 150th Anniversary in 2018.

Above: Rory Bremner came to Kinloch Anderson in 2012 to film for his programme "Great British Views".

Above: Family picture taken at the 150th Anniversary Garden Party in June, 2018.

Left to right: Lachie, Catriona, Isobel, Douglas, Annie, Ken, Ruth (in front), Claire, Deirdre, Douglas, Peter, Ameline, John, Harris, Jo.

generations of its unique family ownership and management. The story is set within the historic events that shaped the future of Kinloch Anderson as tailors and kiltmakers over one hundred and fifty years, and how these have influenced the decisions taken, and the developments which followed, both at home and overseas.

At the time of preparing this book, the United Kingdom was experiencing the damaging uncertainty of Brexit and this was followed by a lockdown as a consequence of the global Covid-19 pandemic. The company had to be closed and the staff put on furlough. It was unprecedented and with life-changing implications for everyone.

Kinloch Anderson has overcome many difficulties arising from worldwide economic, political, environmental and humanitarian problems. The company has survived two world wars, a three-day week, fuel shortages, rationing, economic restrictions and global recessions.

With every setback and every challenge, there comes a new opportunity. Throughout this six-generation story of tailoring and kiltmaking, tartan and Highland Dress, as one door has closed another door has been opened.

I wonder what the next one hundred and fifty years will bring?

ACKNOWLEDGEMENTS

FOR quite some time, I had wanted to write our company's six-generation story. As the project began taking shape, the direction was struggling to emerge and it was my publishers, Waverley Books, who inspired and encouraged me to widen the background into this lifestyle book. My gratitude is immense to Ron Grosset and Liz Small who have assisted me with so much research, knowledge and publishing expertise. Also the cooperative, professional commitments made by the Waverley Books graphic designer, Mark Mechan and editor, Eleanor Abraham, have been outstanding.

I owe so many thanks to my husband Douglas who has been long suffering and whose opinions and company information have been invaluable.

Without my ever-helpful, ever-patient son John and his computer assistance, I could never have managed to complete this book when the coronavirus pandemic required me to self-isolate. I am indebted to John.

I also wish to express my thanks to David Kinloch Anderson for writing the foreword to this book, and to my PA Lee-Anne Mitchell who, until she was furloughed, never faltered from her cheerful and organised approach to the endless chain of emails.

Derek Potter, the former Sovereign's Piper, and Pipe Major with the Royal Scots Dragoon Guards, has been so helpful with regard to his inclusion in the book and the recording of his specially composed pipe music.

There are other family members and business friends who have helped me with the information and the illustrations, most especially my grandson Harris who has taken some of the corporate design and tartan fabric photographs that I wanted to include.

I am most grateful to you all.

PICTURE AND TEXT CREDITS

Many of the images and designs in this book come from the Kinloch Anderson archive and the Kinloch Anderson family collection and are © copyright Kinloch Anderson. A number of images are reproduced from the publication *A Scottish Tradition*, © Kinloch Anderson 2013.

Credits, thanks and acknowledgements for the use of other images and extracts are listed here.

The publishers have made every effort to contact all the copyright holders of the photographs in this book. If we have omitted a credit, we would be glad to hear from you.

Text Sources

Articles and quotes used on pages 39, 53, 54, 55, 70, 103, 104, 105, 115, 118, 119, 120, 121, 134, 202, 209, 210, 212 and 213 are from *The Scotsman* and *Evening News*, are Copyright © The Scotsman Publications and are used with their kind permission.
"The Wall Street Crash", p102 from *Scotland History of a Nation* © David Ross, by permission of Waverley Books.
"The Royal Scots Dragoon Guards", p172–73, courtesy of Brigadier Sir Melville Jameson, KCVO, CBE, CStJ.
"Personal Memoir", p270, courtesy of Pipe Major Derek William James Potter RVM.
Quotes from the Policy Memorandum, the Scottish Register of Tartans Bill, p177–181 © Scottish Parliamentary Corporate Body, 2006.

The publishers acknowledge sources of extracts adapted from works in the public domain, including:
Handbook To Edinburgh – For The Anchor Line, James Middlemass & Co (1872).
The Albert Memorial Guide To Edinburgh, James Middlemass & Co (1877).
Picturesque Edinburgh, by Katherine F Lockie (1899).
Romantic Edinburgh, by John Geddie (1900).
Edinburgh In The Nineteenth Century, Edited by WM Gilbert (1901).
Old & New Edinburgh, by John Geddie (1902).
City of Edinburgh Report on Public Parks, Gardens and Open Spaces, by John W McHattie (1914).
Edinburgh – A Historical Study, by Herbert Maxwell (1916).

Picture Credits

Kinloch Anderson's Scotland Map, p10; © Waverley Books.

Map of North Bridge Street, location 1863, p24; Map of North Bridge Street (detail), p30; Edinburgh & Leith Map – base 1912; reproduced with the permission of the National Library of Scotland, Creative Commons Attribution (CC-BY) licence.

Inset images, Edinburgh & Leith Map, pp 56&57: Sundial: Sandy Gemmill; Scott Monument: contributed; George Watson's College © George Watson's College; Merchiston Castle School: Creative Commons/Kim Traynor; Port of Leith: contributed; George Street: Kinloch Anderson; Register House: Shutterstock/Heartland Arts; John Knox's house: Shutterstock/ArTono; Restalrig: Kinloch Anderson.

Images used under licence from Alamy:
George IV – Keys of Holyrood Palace, p16; The Massed Pipes and Drums, Edinburgh Military Tattoo, August 2019, p179; Eton p205.

Images used under licence from Capital Collections, Edinburgh City Libraries:
The Scott Monument, Archibald Burns,1868, p20; North Bridge Street (Lithograph) by Samuel Dunkinfield Swarbreck, 1837, front endpaper and detail p22; Princes Street, Edinburgh, by Alexander Adam Inglis, p34; Leith Harbour, Thomas Hosmer Shepherd, 1829, rear endpaper.

Images used under licence from Shutterstock:
Front Cover Edinburgh: Gair Brisbane; Back Cover Edinburgh: Songquan Deng; Statue of Sir Walter Scott, p19: Shropshire Matt; Duke of Wellington statue, p46: HeiSpa; Ross Fountain, p47: Javiperhez; Ellen Terry, p49: Morphart Creation; Keir Hardie, p50: Everett Historical; Glasgow Subway, p51: Ondrej_Novotny_92; Inverleith Park, p52: Iordanis; George V, p65 and George V, p82: ale1969; WW1, p90: Everett Historical; John W Mills' "Monument to the Women of World War II", p98: Archer All Square; Charles & Diana, p126: Andy Lidstone; Margaret Thatcher, p126: David Fowler; Mount Everest, p127: Daniel Prudek; European Union Flag, p131: esfera; Riots, p131: a katz; Donald Dewar, p145: Graeme J. Baty; Shanghai–Maglev train, p147: cy obo; The Shore, Leith, p149: Richie Chan; The Royal Yacht Britannia, p151: King Edward VII (1841–1910) in 1903, p155: King Edward VII, p160; King George V, p160; Victoria and Albert, p161; Barack Obama, p196: John Selway; HM

The Queen and HRH Prince Philip, p161: Featureflash; HRH Prince Charles, p161: Jasperimage; George VI, p161: Prachaya Roekdeethaweesab; Balmoral exterior, p162: Traveller70; Register House, p178: Claudine Van Massenhove; World Trade Center, p194: Dan Howell; Hurricane Katrina, p195: Brian Nolan; Facebook symbol, p195: OlegDoroshin; DNA, p195: PopTika; Smartphone, p196: cristo95; Edinburgh Castle fireworks, p197: inspi_ml; Flooded buildings, Brooklyn, p200: FashionStock.com; Icelandic Volcano Eyjafjallajökull, p200: J. Helgason; Edinburgh tram, p200: Spiroview inc; Covid-19 virus graphic, p201: creativeneko; Queensferry Crossing, p201: T.W. van Urk; Abbotsford House, p204: Wapted.

Specific images used by kind permission or arrangement:
Merchant Company images, p79 & 80, Courtesy of the Royal Company of Merchants, Edinburgh; Royal Warrant Holders Association, p80, Courtesy of the Royal Warrant Holders Association; WW2 Uniforms, p96 © Bloomsbury-Osprey, by arrangement; Edinburgh Air Raid Shelter pamphlet and image, public domain; CJ Cousland & Sons Ltd; The Country Shops, p114, by courtesy of Ambaile, Highland History and Culture; The Caledonian Club, London, p149, courtesy of The Caledonian Club; Balmoral interior: "The Drawing Room" (1857), A watercolour by James Roberts (c.1800–1867), p163 © The Royal Collection, by arrangement; Badge of the Royal Scots Dragoon Guards, p171, © The Royal Scots Dragoon Guards, by arrangement; Jamie McGrigor, p178, Great Seal of Scotland, p179 and Committee Room Scottish Parliament, p179 © The Scottish Parliamentary Corporate Body; Bruce Crawford, Minister for Parliamentary Business, and Sir Jamie McGrigor in November 2008, p181 © Alan Milligan; Ronald Kinloch Anderson, p202 © National Portrait Gallery, by arrangement; Robert Masters Quartet, 1950, p203 © Kevin Redshaw; Sir Eric Kinloch Anderson with former Prime Minister Tony Blair, p205 © Tony Harris by arrangement with PA Images. Sundial Restoration, p211, © Graciela Ainsworth, used by kind permission. Sundial Garden Party, pages 212–216 are © Lizzie Hearne, used by kind permission.

Images used under Creative Commons licence:
King George IV landing at Leith in 1822, Alexander Carse (detail), p15; George IV in Highland Dress, p17; Sir Walter Scott, p19; The Clarence, p32; Burke and Hare, p33; Fire of Edinburgh, p33; Queen Victoria, p34; Florence Nightingale, p35; Karl Marx, p35; Singer sewing machine, p46; Horse-drawn bus, c.1900, p46; Tay Bridge, p48; Alexander Graham Bell, p48; The Gowans Sundial (Mafrado), p48; Highland Land League logo, p49; Glasgow Clipper, p49; The Edinburgh International Exhibition,1886, p49; Girl Guide, p65; Harry Lauder, p65; Nancy Astor, p66; St Trinneans School/St Leonard's Hall, p67; Anne Kenney Christabel Pankhurst, p68; General Strike, p68; Amelia Earhart, p69; Ghandi, p69; Wallace Carothers, p69; Crowd at New York's American Union Bank, p74; Map, p90; Crowd outside the New York City Stock Exchange, 1929, p102; Ramsay MacDonald, p102; Winston Churchill, p102; Atomic bomb, p103; The CC41 symbol, p106; Clothing Coupons, p107; Make Do and Mend, p107; BBC Broadcasting House, p108; Forth Road Bridge (M.J. Richardson) p109; Concorde (André Cros), p112; Twin towers of Wembley (Colin Smith), p112; IV fertilisation (Dovidena), p113; 50p coin (Perseus1984), p113; John Lennon (Jack Mitchell), p126; Space Shuttle disaster (NASA), p127; Berlin Wall (Sue Ream), p130; John Major, p130; Nelson Mandela (Paul Weinberg), p144; Stone of Destiny, p144; Queen Victoria, p160; Logo of George VI, p174; Eric Milroy, p207; Scotland XV v France, 1913, p207; The Eric Milroy trophy for kicking (Mémoire Rugby Events), p208.

Contributed images:
Edinburgh from Calton Hill by Myles Birket Foster, p12; Edinburgh's Waverley Station – 1890s, p26; North Bridge (JCH Balmain), Yerbury, p30; 1st Edinburgh City Artillery Volunteers (Grierson) p32; International Exhibition of Industry, Science and Art, 1886, p48; Forth Bridge, p50; The Sundial, Inverleith Park, p51; John W McHattie, p52; The Mound, (Life Jottings), p53; Edinburgh Royal Infirmary, p54; The Town Council of Edinburgh, 1896, (Picturesque Edinburgh), p55; London Illustrated News Masthead, p80; Crowds awaiting King George V and Queen Mary, p81; The Seaforth Highlanders awaiting the procession, p82. Buglers – the Queen's Rifle Volunteer Brigade, 1885, p85; Illustration from Records of the Scottish Volunteer Force (Grierson), p84; Auxiliary Territorial Service, Poster, 1939–1945, p97; Air Raid Precautions poster, from 1939, p98; Clothing coupons, p106; Royal Scots Greys illustration, p171.

Back endpaper:
Leith Harbour, from the pier, by Thomas Hosmer Shepherd, 1829.